The Po the Glory

A Drama in Three Acts

by Dennis Cannan and Pierre Bost

From the Novel by Graham Greene

SAMUEL FRENCH

FOUNDED 1830

New York Hollywood London Toronto

SAMUELFRENCH.COM

THE POWER AND THE GLORY

CHARACTERS

In order of speaking

TENCH, *a dentist*
THE CHIEF OF POLICE
DIAZ, *the dentist's servant*
A PRIEST
A LIEUTENANT OF POLICE
A BOY
MARIA
BRIGITTA, *her daughter*
FRANCISCO
MIGUEL
A POLICEMAN
MESTIZO
THE GOVERNOR'S COUSIN
A DRUNKEN PRISONER
LOPEZ, *another prisoner*
A SPINSTER

THE WARDER
A FARMER'S WIFE
ALVAREZ
VITTORIO, *a muleteer*
A SCHOOLMASTER
OBREGON, *a storekeeper*
OBREGON'S WIFE
RAMON ⎱ *their children*
LOLA ⎰
AN INDIAN
A PEASANT WOMAN
A VILLAGER
AN OLD VILLAGER
A YOUNG WOMAN
A STRANGER

TOWNSPEOPLE, PRISONERS, etc.

THE POWER AND THE GLORY

SCENES

ACT I

ACT II

ACT III

The Power and the Glory

ACT I

SCENE ONE

Outside the dentist's surgery. It is a front scene with openings Right and Left. There is a large window Center on which is written "DENTISTA." There is a street lamp Left and telegraph wire bracket Right. The scene is dark. There are anti-religious posters on the walls.

At RISE OF CURTAIN there are various PEDESTRIANS *passing to and fro. There is a "TART" standing Left and another in the archway Right. A* SAILOR *passes slowly across stage from Right smoking. A* CIVILIAN *enters Right, passing the "TART." He pauses in his stride, ponders for a moment and returns and talks to her. The* SAILOR *talks to the "TART" Left. There is an* OLD MAN *sitting under the window sleeping. Three* POLICEMEN *enter Left. They have torches and they shine them into the faces of passers-by. One* POLICEMAN *crosses over to Right and moves on the* CIVILIAN *and the "TART." A second* POLICEMAN *moves back to the* SAILOR *and* SECOND "TART" *Left and moves them off Left. The third* POLICEMAN *wakes up the* OLD MAN *sleeping under the window— forces him to his feet and pushes him off Left, following him. As they go the LIGHTS fade to out and at the same time BLUES on the back cloth fade in, showing the shadows of* TENCH *CHIEF with forceps in his hand. The street flies out and the LIGHTS fade in as* TENCH *is extracting a tooth.*

(MUSIC is played throughout the scene.)

5

SCENE TWO

*A dentist's surgery. An old-fashioned chair, a cabinet of
drugs and instruments, a spittoon, a work bench. All
the equipment is well worn, the enamel chipped, the
instruments untidy. Cotton wool swabs and magazines lie among the drugs. An opened packing case
is against the wall, and the straw still litters the
floor. An old Southern Railway poster of Bognor is
the only picture. There is a bench along the back
wall for waiting clients. Behind it is a window. A
door Center leads to the street, another Left leads to
the private part of the house.*

TENCH, *the dentist, wears a grubby white coat, stained
under the arms with sweat. He has a button missing
on the front, and a newspaper sticking out of his
pocket. He is attending the* CHIEF OF POLICE, *who
sits in the chair with his mouth full of instruments.
His uniform is untidy and his rucked up trousers
show unsuspended socks. For a while* TENCH *busies
himself with the* CHIEF'S *mouth. A STEAMER
whistles.* TENCH *extracts a tooth.*

TENCH. Rinse. (*Above Right of chair.*)

CHIEF. Ga. (*He empties his mouth into the spittoon.*)
In the end you're as bad as the others.

TENCH. Almost, not quite. (*Examining tooth in forceps.*

CHIEF. Perhaps not quite. (*Looks at tooth.*) And you
do less harm than keeping a rotten tooth.

TENCH. (*Putting tooth in bin Right.*) I do my harm
quicker. One good pull and it's over. That's the principle
of your revolution, isn't it? Tomorrow you'll think no
more about it. (*Crosses Left.*)

CHIEF. About what?

TENCH. Your tooth, of course. Diaz. (DIAZ *enters
Right to Up Center.*) There should be a flagon of ether

and a cylinder of gas on the boat. Go and fetch them. (DIAZ *goes Up Left.* TENCH *looks out of the window towards the boat. The* CHIEF *gargles and spits. BOAT WHISTLE Off. Goes to drawer of cabinet for drill.*) Oh, it used to worry me once. Every time the whistle blew I got the itch to go. The States, then England. Now —I couldn't face the trouble of packing and buying a ticket. Even if I could afford it—

CHIEF. Business bad?

TENCH. It's never been good. Six dentists—and I'm the only one who doesn't carry a gun.

CHIEF. I've got a proposition to put to you. What would you say to becoming the police dentist? Attend our men, and any prisoners in the jail who have to have a tooth drawn. (*Rinse.*)

TENCH. Do you remember that day when you made me draw the tooth of a man condemned to death? The night before his execution. (*Goes Right and attaches drill to machine.*)

CHIEF. That way he could die without suffering. (*Holds his cheek. He gives a rough laugh which doesn't even amuse himself.* TENCH'S *reply is a small sour smile. A short silence.*) Anyway, I haven't shot many—not for a long time. (*Rinse.*)

TENCH. Order reigns. (*Gets wad of cotton wool from shelf Right.*)

CHIEF. I shall be retiring soon. Without too heavy a conscience.

TENCH. And with a few teeth left. (*Open.*)

CHIEF. Well, what about my offer?

TENCH. I suppose you'd want a—a share?

CHIEF. It's usual to pay for concessions.

TENCH. What do you get from the German who does it now?

CHIEF. I can't disclose official contracts.

TENCH. Open, bite. (*He puts cotton wool in corner of his mouth.*) I'd give you thirty per cent. I need the money. Ten years ago I had something in the bank— enough to buy a ticket home and open up in a small way.

Ever heard of Bognor? Why should you have heard of Bognor? Then you had your confounded revolution: (*He commences to pedal and uses drill in* CHIEF's *mouth.*) the peso fell to nothing, and bang went my savings. And here I am stuck in this God-forsaken socialist heaven of yours.

CHIEF. (*Indignantly, his mouth full of steel.*) Ga-ga-ga!

TENCH. I know! I mustn't say anything disrespectful about your revolution. (*The* CHIEF *groans.*) All right, I've nearly finished. You should come more often, then it wouldn't take so long. (*He wipes his eyebrows with his sleeve.*) Ever heard of a cure for sweat? (*Sits stool Right of chair.*)

CHIEF. Ga—wa.

TENCH. (*Cleaning spectacles.*) In this weather my spectacles get so sweated up I can't see through them. Is it true you've put the oculist in jail?

CHIEF. (*With a nod.*) Ah!

TENCH. Crimes against the State?

CHIEF. Ah!

TENCH. You ought to invent something more original. It would make the papers more interesting. "Crimes against the State," (*Rises.*) and no details—it lacks variety. In England on Sundays I used to read a paper called (*Takes mouth mirror and examines* CHIEF's *mouth.*) "News of the World." You'd be surprised what people get arrested for in a democracy. A little wider— (*He takes some cotton wool out of the* CHIEF's *mouth.*) There you are. You'd better come back next week for scaling.

CHIEF. You bruised me round here. It's aching worse than before.

TENCH. It'll wear off. (*Crosses Left.*) I'll give you something to ease it. (*He fills a beaker from a bottle.*)

CHIEF. What?

TENCH. Oil of cloves.

CHIEF. Oil of cloves! In the old days you would have given me a glass of brandy. Do you remember the good old days before prohibition—real Vera Cruz—real French brandies. Henessey. Give me your oil of cloves. (*Takes a sip and is about to spit into the spittoon. Then he stops and swallows with relish. His expression changes. He beams, licks his lips and takes a gulp.*) Aha! (*Whispering.*) This didn't come through the Customs.

TENCH. I got some sent with my plaster of Paris. For medicinal purposes.

CHIEF. (*With a snigger.*) I should arrest you for this.

TENCH. (*Crosses to door Up Left Center.*) I should report you to the Governor for drinking it.

CHIEF. Don't blame the Governor. I've seen his cellar. Real French wines—all confiscated, of course. (*He sips.*) Aren't you drinking?

TENCH. (*Crosses to wash basin Left.*) No. I'm not interested any longer. Oh, I used to take—restoratives for years. But when one takes restoratives, it's because one wants to be restored—to something. (*Washes hands.*)

CHIEF. I'm sorry. I thought—

TENCH. You do me too much honor. I don't drink any more, I don't drug any more. Women (*He makes a little gesture.*) I don't even play at billiards. (*To Center.*)

CHIEF. You shouldn't have given up billiards. Even my lieutenant has got nothing against billiards.

TENCH. (*Taking towel from* CHIEF *and folding it.*) Your new Lieutenant sees wrong everywhere. It's a habit strong men have. Don't retire yet, will you?

CHIEF. Why? (*Rises, goes up Left for gun-belt.*)

TENCH. Because he'll replace you. And at my age I can't stomach strong men. (*Puts towel over back of chair. In a serious puzzled voice as though he is really giving away a secret.*) Do you know what was the restorative I hid here longest? Religion. I didn't think I had it in me. (*Goes Right and picks up bin.*)

CHIEF. (*Very serious too, now.*) Be careful. Don't go too far. (*Puts on belt.*)

TENCH. (*Emptying bin into stove Down Right.*) Oh, I've kept it only as long as it was illegal. Now I've rid myself of that too. I don't want to be shot like a priest or burnt like a church.

CHIEF. You'd better not say that to the Lieutenant. (*Looks in mirror Down Left.*)

TENCH. I'm not a fool. Anyway, it wasn't your Holy Roman Church. Only a belief in Something, Somewhere. Now I believe in Nothing and Nowhere.

(*The door opens and the* PRIEST *enters Up Center. He wears a dilapidated black suit and carries a small attache case.*)

PRIEST. (*Left Center—a little breathless.*) Are you the dentist?

TENCH. As you see. (*Back of chair.*)

PRIEST. (*Seeming to choose his words.*) I have an old filling which has worked loose. It needs attention.

TENCH. (*Glances at the* CHIEF'S *back. He makes a little sign of caution.*) Sit down. Can't you see I'm attending to the Chief of Police?

(*The* PRIEST *starts. He sits down anxiously Up Center. A pause. The* CHIEF *has finished his brandy. He rings the glass suggestively.* TENCH *goes Left.*)

CHIEF. That "oil of cloves" is just the stuff. The ache's almost gone— (TENCH *takes no notice.*) Come on, now —there's no shortage of "oil of cloves"—is there? (TENCH *refills the beaker Left. The* CHIEF *can hardly contain his laughter. Wiping his eyes.*) Aha! Ho! Oh, you're a lucky fellow.

TENCH. Why?

CHIEF. Being a foreigner.

TENCH. I'm not a foreigner. I'm English. (*Handing him refilled glass.*)

(*SIREN. While he talks, we notice an exchange of glances between* TENCH *and the* PRIEST. *Now the*

CHIEF *remembers that there is a stranger present.
He drinks his brandy and changes his tone.*)

CHIEF. (*Glass on dental table, goes Up Right for cap.*)
It's a long time since I've seen you at the cantina. You
ought to take up billiards again. (*The STEAMER
WHISTLE blows. The* PRIEST *gets up and looks anxiously through the window. Then he looks desperately
at* TENCH, *who is putting away his instruments.*) Well,
how about tonight?

TENCH. What?

CHIEF. Billiards.

TENCH. Perhaps you're right.

CHIEF. (*Takes a look at the* PRIEST.) Who are you? A
school teacher?

PRIEST. (*Rises.*) I sell medicine.

CHIEF. A doctor? (*Puts foot on bench.*) You can tell
me what's wrong with my bowels. Every morning—

PRIEST. I'm not qualified. I'm not allowed to practise.

CHIEF. A quack? (*The* PRIEST *nods humbly.*) Be careful. We've had too many quacks selling tooth powder to
the Indians and saying they'll live for ever. The Lieutenant is strict with your kind. (*To the* DENTIST, *crossing
Left Center.*) Tonight.

TENCH. At seven.

CHIEF. And then I will take my revenge. (*Leaves Left
Center.*)

TENCH. Sit down. I can't give you much time.

PRIEST. Didn't I get it right? (*Sits dental chair,* TENCH
puts towel on his neck.)

TENCH. Tell me again what's wrong. Exactly. (*Right
of chair.*)

PRIEST. I have an old filling which has worked loose.
It needs attention.

TENCH. Where?

PRIEST. The upper incisor. (*A pause. Tench looks with
mouth mirror.*)

TENCH. Open. (*Pause.*) You're late. Gonzales told me

to expect you last night. (*He puts mirror on table and closes blind—then lowers door blind.*)

PRIEST. I didn't want to be seen about the town.

TENCH. You've cut it very fine. Your boat's ready to go. (*To cabinet Left.*)

PRIEST. Have you got the papers?

TENCH. All in order—ticket—embarkation permit. You must fill it in in your own handwriting. (*Puts passport and permit on table.*)

PRIEST. Have you a pen?

TENCH. I used to have one. (*He searches cabinet.*) In the days when I kept records and wrote letters. (*He brings pen and ink to* PRIEST.) You'll have to stay here now. The Police always search the boat before it sails.

PRIEST. There's not much time. I heard a siren just now.

TENCH. There are three sirens. Wait for the third one, then get on board in the last rush. Here. Your name is Miguel Lopez.

PRIEST. My hand—it's the excitement—

TENCH. You're going to Vera Cruz—

PRIEST. It's so long since I held a pen.

TENCH. —on business connected with the import of cement. (*Takes paper and dries it by heat from stove.*)

PRIEST. Thank you. Would you care for a glass of brandy? (*He opens his case and takes out bottle.*)

TENCH. Where did you get it? It's no business of mine. I don't drink anyway. (*The* PRIEST *is about to take the rinsing glass by the chair when* TENCH *stops him.*) Not that. (*He takes a water receptacle from his cabinet and wipes it with a cloth.*)

PRIEST. Brandy is a good dentist. (TENCH *does not respond. Apologetically.*) In my profession one makes little pleasantries, it becomes a habit—to make people laugh—sometimes they do laugh. (TENCH *hands him glass; he pours.*)

TENCH. (*Coldly.*) In your profession? I don't like quacks. I believe in diplomas. (*Puts paper on table.*)

PRIEST. I'm not—exactly a quack. I'm a traveller for a pharmacy.

TENCH. You are, are you? (*Suddenly.*) Let's see your samples. (*Puts out a hand to the case and the* PRIEST *whips it away.*)

PRIEST. (*Gravely.*) Perhaps I am a quack. A bit of one.

TENCH. Have you got a cure for this country, Quack?

PRIEST. Only this.

TENCH. 30 under proof. I need something stronger— a ticket.

PRIEST. Why do you stay?

TENCH. I haven't enough cash to go. Go where?

PRIEST. Home?

TENCH. What home? My wife remarried a long time ago. Not her fault. I hadn't written for five years.

PRIEST. Have you any children? (*Drinks.*)

TENCH. Yes, two. Somewhere. Have you?

PRIEST. (*A short silence. He empties his glass and fills another.*) I have a daughter.

TENCH. Are you leaving her behind?

PRIEST. Yes.

TENCH. I wouldn't leave a dog here.

PRIEST. I've never seen her.

TENCH. You've never——? Oh, well, it's none of my business. How did you pay Gonzales for your ticket? In gold?

PRIEST. Yes. He insisted.

TENCH. Where did you get it?

PRIEST. I had—something made of gold.

TENCH. A watch?

PRIEST. Something made of gold.

(*KNOCK.* PRIEST *puts bottle in case.* TENCH *covers papers, pen and ink with towel, and opens door blind. Enter the* LIEUTENANT. *He is smartly turned out, young, efficient.*)

LIEUT. From Police Headquarters. Are you Tench the dentist?

TENCH. Yes, Lieutenant. I know you—by sight. (*To Left of chair.*)

LIEUT. You have fewer faces to remember. Are you busy? (*Left Center.*)

TENCH. Just finished. (*Picking up papers under towel —to the* PRIEST.) Feeling better?

PRIEST. Thank you. Yes. How much do I owe you? (*Going to Left of* TENCH.)

TENCH. Pay me next time. You'll have to come back. (*Puts papers still under towel on table Up Right.*)

(*The* PRIEST, *holding his jaw, goes out into the street. Second hoot from SIREN.*)

LIEUT. You've hurt him? (*Hanging hat up Left.*)

TENCH. Sometimes you can't help it.

LIEUT. A pity. The Chief of Police recommended you as the best dentist in town. (*Crosses to chair.*)

TENCH. That's no compliment. But it's the truth. You want to consult me?

LIEUT. Yes. (*Sitting in the chair and examining the equipment.*) Not very up-to-date.

TENCH. It was, when I started. (*Puts towel from cabinet drawer round his neck.*)

LIEUT. Ten years ago?

TENCH. (*Picking up his probe.*) Nearly twelve. (*Pumps dental chair up.*)

LIEUT. So you're pre-revolution.

TENCH. (*Trying to start his examination.*) M'm.

LIEUT. Ever thought that you wanted to get back to England?

TENCH. Of course.

LIEUT. Waiting till you've made a fortune?

TENCH. Not much chance. Not with your taxes. What did you want to see me about?

LIEUT. I need a bridge.

TENCH. Open. (*With mouth mirror making his examination.*) At the bottom on the right? (*The* LIEUTENANT *grunts.* TENCH *goes* L.) How did you lose the tooth? Accident?

LIEUT. Argument.

TENCH. You'd be wasting your money. I can fill the gap without a bridge.

LIEUT. I'd prefer a bridge.

TENCH. Just as you like. (*He takes some samples from a drawer.*) Choose your style. This one looks natural. (*To table with samples.*)

LIEUT. (*After picking over the samples.*) No. I want it in gold.

TENCH. (*On his guard.*) I'm not allowed to make gold teeth. You know it as well as I do. All gold is the property of the State.

LIEUT. So you can't plead ignorance.

TENCH. What do you mean?

LIEUT. (*Puts towel in chair—rises—to Left of* TENCH, *a hand in his pocket.*) What I wanted was something like—this— (*He holds a gold tooth.* TENCH *takes it.*) You know what it is?

TENCH. A gold tooth. If you don't mind breaking the law—

LIEUT. It isn't mine.

TENCH. (*Handing it back.*) In that case—

LIEUT. It's yours. Surely you remember? It's well-made—your own work.

TENCH. From time to time I've obliged a patient who's been able to give me the gold. Officials. (*Back to cabinet with samples.*)

LIEUT. Who is Gonzales? (*Putting tooth on table.*)

TENCH. (*Taken off his guard.*) Gonzales?

LIEUT. You should know. You made him that tooth. We arrested him last night.

TENCH. What for?

LIEUT. Dealing in gold. (*Crossing behind chair to stove.*) And other things: forging papers. . . . Dentists have equipment for melting metal. Is that how you were useful to Gonzales?

TENCH. (*Left.*) Anyone can make a furnace—

LIEUT. (*Right.*) We didn't find one at Gonzales' house. But we found other things he hadn't had time to bring you. A gold chalice.

TENCH. A chalice?

LIEUT. (*Above chair.*) Only a priest could have given him that. A priest. This isn't trafficking in gold. It's treason. I shot two hostages at Saltas yesterday. Do you think I'd spare you, when we kill our own people?

TENCH. I'm sure you wouldn't. What did you shoot them for? (*Crossing Right, puts bits of cotton wool in stove.*)

LIEUT. We found wine buried under a hut.

TENCH. You shot two men for a bottle of wine?

LIEUT. Yes.

TENCH. (*To behind chair.*) What's the punishment for brandy? Your Chief's fond of it.

LIEUT. They can make beasts of themselves with brandy for all I care. It's what they do with the wine— and bread—

TENCH. You haven't forbidden us to eat bread, have you? They say you can hear Mass still in Mexico City. And in Vera Cruz. And in Chiapas.

LIEUT. Every other state in Mexico may break the law. I'll see we keep it here. (*He picks up the tooth.*) You'll get no more gold from Gonzales. (*Crossing Down Left.*)

TENCH. Is he dead?

LIEUT. Yes. (DIAZ *enters Up Center with the ether and cylinder from the street. Puts them under cabinet Down Left.*) Diaz? You remember me?

DIAZ. Yes, Lieutenant. (*Right of him.*)

LIEUT. Is all going well with you here? (*Left of him.*)

DIAZ. I try to do my best.

LIEUT. I found you the job. Don't let me down. Is your wife working?

DIAZ. She was cleaning the hotel, Lieutenant, but they say she must go.

LIEUT. Why's that?

DIAZ. They say they only want help when the boat comes in—three or four days every month.

LIEUT. Tell her to come to the barracks and ask for me. I'll try to find her something. (*Goes up Left for cap.*)

DIAZ. (*Gratefully.*) Oh, Lieutenant—

LIEUT. I can't promise, but tell her I'll try.

DIAZ. Thank you, Lieutenant. (*Crosses Right and goes into inner room.*)

LIEUT. (*At door.*) A priest would hear their confessions and tell them to reform. It's more use to find them work. (*At the door.*) Report to my office at the barracks in an hour's time. Bring your passport with you—and your permit to practise.

(*He goes into the street.* TENCH *switches off lights, closes blind, goes quickly to the window. The* PRIEST *edges through the door, looking in the direction taken by the* LIEUTENANT.)

PRIEST. He's gone to the ship.

TENCH. What was it you gave to Gonzales?

PRIEST. Oh—just a family possession.

TENCH. You're a liar! (*The* PRIEST *says nothing.*) D' you think I run this Cook's agency out of charity or conviction? (*To Left of* PRIEST.) I'll help any bum to get out of the country if it helps to pay my passage back home—but a priest! Take your ticket and get to hell out of here. (*Goes Up Right.*) Father, Monseigneur, Eminence. They've found your chalice. Gonzales is dead. (*He gets ticket from under towel.*)

PRIEST. Dead?

TENCH. Give me your case. (TENCH *snatches the bag out of the* PRIEST'S *hand and pulls it open. He pulls out a book. Throws ticket on floor.*) A missal. You fool, to carry that around. I won't die for you like Gonzales. (*He stuffs the missal in the stove. The* PRIEST *stands by.*)

PRIEST. (*In sudden fear.*) Are you going to give me up?

TENCH. (*To him.*) You're not only a drunk and a coward. You are a sickness. People die from contact with you.

PRIEST. (*Pleading.*) I shall be gone in a few minutes now.

TENCH. Don't think I wouldn't give you up, but it's too late. They've seen you with me. (*He gets up and goes back to the window.*) Here he comes again. Get back. No, there. (*The* PRIEST *goes* L. *Then towards door* R., *puts his hand on the inner door.*) No, my man's there. Sit down there and pray, damn you, pray. (PRIEST *sits dental chair. A long pause.* TENCH *relaxes.*) He's turned the corner. Now get out. Here are your papers. (*Picks them up— gives them.*) Go. The quicker the better for everybody. Go and hang yourself elsewhere.

PRIEST. I'm sorry. You've been very kind. (*He holds out his hand but* TENCH *refuses to take it.*) God help you. (*Kneels Left Center, re-packing case.*)

TENCH. Let Him help you. *You* belong to Him, not me.

(*Neither of them notices the door open slowly. A small*
BOY *stands looking in.*)

BOY. (*To Left of* TENCH. *Both* MEN *start.*) Are you the doctor?

TENCH. What are you doing here?

BOY. Are you the doctor?

TENCH. Why? Have you got a pain?

BOY. It's my mother.

TENCH. What's wrong with her?

BOY. She's sick.

(*The hunted look comes back to the* PRIEST'S *face. He is
not looking at the* BOY.)

TENCH. (*Up* R. *by window.*) I'm not a doctor. I'm a dentist. I only attend to people's teeth. (DIAZ *enters Right and exits Left Center.*) Diaz, go and stand by the gangway when the last siren goes and the rush starts, wave your hand. Go on. Do as you're told.

BOY. They said there was a doctor here.

TENCH. Where have you come from?

BOY. Helcatoyan.

TENCH. How did you get here?

BOY. On my father's mule.

TENCH. If you wanted a doctor, you should have gone to Yajalon. I can't help you. What's wrong with your mother?

BOY. She has fever.

TENCH. So does everyone at this time of year.

BOY. They say she's dying.

TENCH. (*Shrugs, and looks out of the window.*) All clear. Go on—hurry. Out that way and through the yard.

(*With a sudden frenzy the* PRIEST *pockets the papers and snatches up his case. The* BOY *runs to Right of him.*)

BOY. (*A great hope.*) Are *you* the doctor?

PRIEST. No! No! He's more a doctor than I am.

BOY. (*To Left of him.*) She's dying. I know she's dying. (*A pause. The* PRIEST *looks at the* BOY *with fury.*)

TENCH. (*Trying to hurry the* PRIEST.) What are you waiting for? (PRIEST *pauses—then goes up to door.* BOY *runs up and bars his way.*)

BOY. When she looks at me she doesn't know me any more.

(*THREE SIRENS. The anger goes out of the* PRIEST. *He is suddenly tired and old and resigned. He puts his papers in the stove and gives his attache case to the* BOY.)

PRIEST. Put this case on your mule. (BOY *exits. To* TENCH *wearily.*) They always say they're dying . . . (*Exits Center.*)

BLACKOUT

SCENE THREE

Outside the dentist's surgery. The two "TARTS" are in
their places. There are the usual passers-by. A
CIVILIAN crosses to "TART" and talks to her, Left.
A small CRIPPLE BOY enters slowly from Left. He
moves to Left Center. The "TART" and the CIVILIAN
move off Left. The stage remains empty except for
the CRIPPLE BOY. He looks furtively to Right and
to Left. He takes some chalk from his pocket and
draws a crucifix on the wall Left of the window. He
moves to Center. Again he looks round, crouches
down and on the wall under the window he chalks
the word "CRISTO." As he does so, two POLICE-
MEN enter from Right and ONE from Left. They
pause and watch him for a moment. They then begin
to close in on him. As the BOY gets to the end of
the word, one POLICEMAN from Right takes revolver
from his holster and with the butt-end he hits the
BOY as they all THREE converge on him. The BOY
with a cry collapses. They pick him up and move
off Left with him.

BLACKOUT

(MUSIC is played throughout.)

SCENE FOUR

A hut in the village a month later. A door, roughly Cen-
ter, leads outside. Beside it is a window. Another
door, Right, leads to the bedroom. A cook stove, pots
and pans, rough furniture. It is late evening and too
dark to see the details. We cannot even see the MAN
crouched asleep on the chair beside the inner door.
MARIA, a peasant woman, is hanging washing on line

Left Center. She calls: "Brigitta" three times with pauses. A man enters doorway. It is the PRIEST. *He is in peasant's clothes, barefooted.* MARIA *turns and sees him.*

MARIA. (*Sharply.*) Who's that? Who are you? (*Crossing to him.*)

PRIEST. Don't you know me, Maria? (*In doorway.*)

MARIA. You, Father?

PRIEST. (*Sadly.*) You didn't recognize me. I've changed, haven't I? You haven't. (*Crosses to Left Center.*)

(*A short silence.* MARIA *greets the* PRIEST *without pleasure but with a certain respect. Her words are hard but they are not said in anger. They are the words of a woman very exhausted who wants nothing but quiet. Sometimes in them there is a shade of rather bitter irony.*)

MARIA. What are you doing here? You know it isn't safe.

PRIEST. (*Sits, exhausted, on stool Left Center.*) I'd like to eat a little, then rest a day or two.

MARIA. (*Shakes her head.*) You can't do that, Father. You can eat a little and sleep a little, but then you must go as quickly as possible. (*Puts food on table.*)

PRIEST. Are you afraid?

MARIA. I'm not, but the others. You've been at Helcatoyan.

PRIEST. Yes, I went there to give the sacrament to a dying woman. When I got there, she was no more dying than I am. A bad conscience takes any pain for death. Even a little fever.

MARIA. (*Right of him.*) You heard what happened afterwards?

PRIEST. No. (*He lifts a foot and shows the sores on his sole.*) You see, I've been travelling.

MARIA. They learnt you had been there. They shot two hostages.

PRIEST. (*After a pause.*) If somebody talks, is it my fault? Do you think I wanted to go to Helcatoyan? I had a passage on a boat a month ago. You would never have seen me again if a mosquito hadn't bitten an old woman.

MARIA. (*Hanging up shawl Down Right.*) The people don't want you. They're afraid. (*Then crosses Up Right for bread from cupboard.*)

PRIEST. (*Suddenly angry and trying to assert his dignity.*) I tell you I'm staying here, Maria! I'm going to see my daughter. And I shall speak to the people. I shall say Mass. This is not the way to receive a priest. I'm still a priest, Maria. (*Violently.*) I shall say Mass.

MARIA. They don't want it. (*Puts bread on table.*)

PRIEST. (*Sternly.*) Whether they want it or not.

MARIA. You haven't the right.

PRIEST. It's a long time since I've eaten. Thank you, Maria. I must say Mass quickly so that I can eat.

(*The curtain opens furtively.*)

MARIA. (*Roughly.*) Where have you been?

(BRIGITTA *enters. She is a small girl of ten years or less with a secret calm assurance. She remains on the threshold. The* PRIEST *watches her. His hands tremble.* BRIGITTA *looks back at him with cold eyes, calmly, without expression.* MARIA *appears nervous and wants to cut the scene short. She moves towards* BRIGITTA, *but the* PRIEST *holds her back by the sleeve. He is very moved by the sight of his daughter.*)

PRIEST. Brigitta. (*To* MARIA.) Leave her alone. (MA-RIA *gives way with bad grace. The* PRIEST *lets go of* MARIA *and goes towards* BRIGITTA. *He tries to put his hand on the head of the child, but* BRIGITTA *avoids him. The* PRIEST, *embarrassed, tries to coax* BRIGITTA, *but he is very maladroit.*) Don't be afraid, Brigitta. You're not afraid, are you? (BRIGITTA *is silent. Goes Down Right then crosses to table.*)

MARIA. (*Roughly.*) Go on, say something!

PRIEST. Let her be, Maria, let her be. (BRIGITTA *is close to the table on which the bread is placed. She looks at it. Puts her hand on the bread. Jokingly.*) Are you hungry? (*He puts out his hand but* BRIGITTA *again avoids him and seizes the bread.*)

MARIA. Brigitta—

BRIGITTA. It doesn't belong to him.

PRIEST. (*Quiets* MARIA *with a gesture and moves towards* BRIGITTA. *Softly.*) It belongs to your mother. But she has given it to me. You can look after it if you want to. (BRIGITTA *hugs the bread against her breast. Down Left.*) See this coin—I say the magic words—and then I do that—and it's gone. Watch. ABRA-CADABRA—one, two, three. (*He chooses a coin.*) I'm not so good at it now. (*The trick misfires and he drops the coin. He kneels and finds coin.*) I must practise more. But I haven't many coins. And perhaps you're too old for conjuring tricks. . . . Do you know your catechism? Who made you? (*Sits Center stool.* BRIGITTA *moves round to Right of him.*)

MARIA. She knows it, but she won't say it.

PRIEST. Why not? Why won't you say it? God wants you to—

BRIGITTA. What do you know about God?

MARIA. You little devil—get— (*Left of* BRIGITTA. *She is about to strike her. But the* PRIEST *catches her hand.*)

PRIEST. No!

MARIA. I'm her mother, aren't I? Go on, get outside. (*She takes bread from her and pushes her out, then turns back towards the* PRIEST. *She says with bitter weariness.*) You see what the child's like. They all avoid her. Who can blame them? She's wicked.

PRIEST. A child can't be wicked.

MARIA. You know well enough there's a curse on a priest's child.

PRIEST. Not on the child.

MARIA. Yes, on the child, on me, on you. (*Crosses, puts bread on table.*) There's nothing we can do. (*Sits stool Down Left.*)

PRIEST. You've got to try.

MARIA. It does no good.

PRIEST. (*Moves away from* MARIA. *Her words have stung him and he speaks with an angry violence.*) It does no good! That's what everyone says all the time. It does no good. (*Rise to behind table.*) Only the police and the enemies of God believe that something does good. And that's why they do something. (*Short silence.*) I'm going to say Mass. I am going to say Mass. Hurry. (*Lowering his voice in an appeal.*) I'm faint for food. I know one must fast, but not for three days. (*Sits stool Left Center.*)

MARIA. (*To the* PRIEST.) Stay where you are. (*Crosses to doorway.*) Well?

(*The curtain opens and* FRANCISCO *enters.*)

FRANCISCO. Is it true the Father's here?

MARIA. How did you know?

FRANCISCO. Brigitta told us. (*Crosses to* PRIEST.)

(MARIA *crosses Left to above table.* TWO OTHERS *join him in the doorway, a young man,* MIGUEL, *and an* OLD WOMAN. *All villagers enter and stand silently looking at* PRIEST.)

MARIA. What do you want?

MIGUEL. We want him to go.

(*More people arrive all the time and press into the room. The* PRIEST *moves forward and they recognize him. A silence.* PRIEST *holds out his hand to the* OLD WOMAN *who unwillingly curtseys and kisses it.*)

OLD WOMAN. (*Coming forward.*) Will you say Mass, Father? (*Kisses his hand.*)

PRIEST. Yes, I will. Now. Candles, Maria, and a clean cloth on the table.

MIGUEL. It's too dangerous.

OLD WOMAN. It's been a long time.

YOUNG MAN. She's old. The old don't have to be afraid.

2ND VOICE. That's true. We have our lives still, Father.

PEASANT WOMAN. It's six years since we heard a Mass.

MAN. It's safer for all of us if he goes now.

PRIEST. Do you all want me to go? (*Silence. Rises to Center.*) You know me here. You know what kind of a priest I am. All the same I can give you His body and His blood. If you tell me to go I'll go away. But He'll go too. Shall I go? (*Silence.*) Then we stay—He and I. Maria, my case. (MARIA *gets it. He opens his case and takes out a bottle of wine.*)

FRANCISCO. (*To his Right.*) Have you everything you need, Father?

PRIEST. Practically nothing that I need, but God knows that. (*To* MARIA.) Maria, the cloth and candles.

(MARIA *reluctantly obeys, helped by* FRANCISCO. MIGUEL *approaches the* PRIEST. *He is embarrassed.*)

MIGUEL. (*Right.*) Father, it would be better—it's too dangerous for you.

PRIEST. For me?

MIGUEL. They'll finish by catching you. You would do much better to go north. Past the frontier to Chiapas.

MAN. Be reasonable, Father. The churches are open there.

PRIEST. I've wanted to be reasonable. I was going to leave. But God made me miss my boat, so here I am. (*While he speaks,* MARIA, *helped by* FRANCISCO, *has laid the cloth on the table, and the two candles. The* PRIEST *turns to her, Center.*) Give me a glass, Maria.

MARIA. I haven't a glass, Father—a cup. (*Goes to cupboard for cup.*)

PRIEST. That will do.

MIGUEL. (*Insistently.*) You've got to understand us. If they find you here, they'll burn the village.

PRIEST. (*Replies to* MIGUEL *without anger. He is explaining for the others as much as for* MIGUEL.) Yes, if I go away, you'll be quiet here. And in this whole State it will be as if God did not exist. Can you imagine a place where God does not exist at all? Oh, I know I'm not the best one to show you and your children what the Church means. But isn't a bad priest better than no priest at all?

MIGUEL. Perhaps.

PRIEST. (*Dryly.*) Not perhaps. (*He looks round him. Two more* VILLAGERS *enter.*) This won't be a grand Mass, and not a very long one. But it will be a Mass all the same. God will be here. Take your places. Francisco, make the collection. This is for me. I have to live. I have to buy wine. Wine is illegal. I have to bribe—for your sakes. (FRANCISCO *makes the collection. Some kneel, the others remain standing.*) I haven't a missal left, and I don't know what the day is. No missal, no chalice, no vestments, no altar stone. Only a little bread and a little wine. But that's all God needs. He doesn't depend on a rich church and fine statues and gold thread in the vestments. (FRANCISCO *gives him the collection.*) You're poor. But there is no wealth greater than to be poor. My children, one of the Fathers of the Church has told us that joy always depends on pain. Pain is part of joy. When we are hungry we feel already the joy of food. Before we marry, we deny ourselves through the long betrothal. . . . (*He puts coins in his pocket. His eye meets* MARIA'S *as he stops defensively, expecting a laugh.*) That is why I tell you that Heaven is here; your suffering is a part of Heaven, just as pain is a part of pleasure. Never get tired of suffering. The police watching you, the soldiers gathering taxes, the smallpox and fever, hunger—that is the beginning of Heaven, without them Heaven would not be complete. And Heaven, what is Heaven? Heaven is where there are no unjust laws, no taxes, no soldiers and no hunger. You will never be afraid there—or unsafe. Nobody grows old. The crops never fail. Oh,

it's easy to say all the things that there will *not* be in
Heaven. What is there is God, and we have no words for
Him. In the name of the Father, the Son and the Holy
Ghost, Amen. Now I am going to say Mass.

(*A man stands as "look-out" outside the hut. The* PRIEST
*turns back towards the table and begins to say the
Mass. He says only the Canon so as to shorten the
ceremony. As he consecrates the wine—the* LOOK-
OUT *rushes in.* ALL *turn.*)

MAN. Father—they are only a mile off riding out of
the forest.
PRIEST. (*Turns to the congregation.*) Remember
Heaven is here. Now, at this moment. Your fear and my
fear are part of Heaven. How long have we got?
MAN. Three minutes, Father, not a second longer.
PRIEST. Time enough. (*He turns back to altar.*)
MARIA. It's safer to stay here. If they see people running, they'll shoot. (*The* PRIEST *turns back to the altar.
He consecrates and eats the bread very quickly, then he
consecrates the wine in the cup. The* PRIEST *drinks the
wine quickly. Moves Right Center.* FRANCISCO, *aided by
the others, undresses the altar, removing anything that
might suggest the Mass. While they do this,* MARIA *approaches the* PRIEST.) Breathe, breathe on me. (*He does.*)
You smell of wine. (*She goes to the cupboard. Comes
back to him and hands him something.*) Eat this onion.
(*The* PRIEST *eats the onion.*)

(BRIGITTA *enters, goes up Center.*)

MAN. They're getting closer.

(*The* VILLAGERS *stand round the room,* PRIEST *Down
Left. The* LIEUTENANT *enters, followed by a* SOL-
DIER. *The* LIEUTENANT *is tired, he has flashes of
anger when he speaks, but usually his voice seems
to contain the desire to convince these people of his*

good intentions. He walks all round the room, taking
everything in. Then he stops in the middle, stuck
there like a hard rock.)

LIEUT. What are you all doing here? Why aren't you
in your fields?

MARIA. (*Up Left Center.*) We were talking about the
drought.

LIEUT. You were saying your morning prayers. Do you
think I don't know it? (*He picks out a* MAN *Right to*
question.) Have you seen a stranger here?

THE MAN. (*Confused.*) A stranger?

LIEUT. Any newcomer in the village?

THE MAN. No, Lieutenant.

LIEUT. (*To* ANOTHER—*Up Left.*) You, there, tell me,
have you seen a man come from the direction of Helcatoyan?

THE MAN. Helcatoyan? I don't know anyone at Helcatoyan.

LIEUT. (*Down Left to a* WOMAN.) You, tell me where
he is.

WOMAN. I have seen nobody, Lieutenant.

LIEUT. So nobody has seen anyone? (*To Down Center.*
He suddenly cries out like an order.) Attention, and
listen! I'm not here for the sake of a ride. I'm here because I'm looking for a priest. The last priest—and I've
given my word I'll take him before the rains. (*Sits stool*
Center. Takes off cap. A pause.) Anyone who gives him
refuge or speaks to him or even sees him without report-
ing to me are enemies of the State, and they'll be shot.
So if any of you have seen him, speak. (*A silence. The*
LIEUTENANT *watches them. Rise.*) There's a reward of
seven hundred pesos. (*They remain silent. He goes round*
table Up Left. The LIEUTENANT *is taken by a wave of*
anger.) Has a priest ever offered you seven hundred
pesos? What have they ever done for you, the priests?
All they want is your money. What has God ever done
for you? Have you got enough to eat? Have your children got enough to eat? Instead of food they talk to you

about Heaven. Oh, everything will be fine after you are dead, but I tell you everything will be fine for you here, in your own time and your children's time, when there are no more priests to take your money. You have to buy your heaven up there. We give it to you down here. But you must help us. (*Again a silence, and he goes on more calmly.*) At Helcatoyan I took hostages, and now they are dead. From here too I shall take a hostage; if I learn the priest has passed by here, the hostage dies. And don't make any mistake. If the priest has come here I shall learn it. Sooner or later there is always someone who talks. Someone who wants your piece of land—or your cow. (*Another* SOLDIER *appears Right. Goes to* LIEUTEN-ANT. LIEUTENANT *questions him.*) Nothing in the village?

SOLDIER. Nothing.

LIEUT. No trace?

SOLDIER. We found nothing, Lieutenant. (*Breaks Up Left.*)

LIEUT. (*The* LIEUTENANT *turns back towards the crowd. He is almost a suppliant now. Goes Right to Down Right then to Center.*) Why don't you trust me? (*A pause.*) There is no need even to speak if he's here among you. Just look at him. (*Stands Down Center, back to audience.*) No one will know then that it was you who gave him away. He won't know himself—if you are afraid of his curses. (*He looks round the villagers.* EVERY-BODY *looks at the ground. Suddenly the* LIEUTENANT *has had enough of it. He points at* FRANCISCO.) Take him. (*Two* SOLDIERS *quickly hold the young man. Exit with him Right.*)

WOMAN. It's my son!

LIEUT. Everyone here is a son or a father or a husband of somebody. (*To the* SOLDIERS.) Take him away. (*They go out—*WOMAN *follows.*)

PRIEST. (*Crosses Left Center.*) Lieutenant— (EVERY-ONE *watches the* PRIEST *in silence.*) Take me. I'm sick. I'm not good for anything.

LIEUT. (*Right Center—dryly.*) Then you're no good for a hostage. (*As the* PRIEST *turns away, the* LIEUTEN-

ANT *calls after him.*) Wait. Come here. What's your name? (*Crosses below to his Left.*)

PRIEST. Montez.

LIEUT. What do you do?

PRIEST. I have a little land.

LIEUT. Are you married?

PRIEST. Yes.

LIEUT. Which is your wife?

MARIA. (*Breaking out.*) I am. Why do you ask so many questions? Do you think. he looks like a priest?

LIEUT. Let me see your hands. (*The PRIEST holds them up. They are as hard as a laborer's. Suddenly the LIEUTENANT leans forward and sniffs at his breath. There is complete silence among the VILLAGERS, a dangerous silence that seems to convey their fear to the LIEUTEN-ANT. A pause.*) All right, get back. (*As the PRIEST turns.*) Wait! (*To BRIGITTA.*) Come here! (*BRIGITTA sidles forward.*) You know everyone in this village, don't you? (*BRIGITTA nods. Left Center.*) Who's that man there? What's his name? (*Center.*)

BRIGITTA. I don't know.

LIEUT. (*Sharply.*) You don't know his name? Is he a stranger?

MARIA. (*Up Left Center.*) The child doesn't know her own name. Ask her who her father is.

LIEUT. Who's your father? (*BRIGITTA points at the PRIEST. LIEUTENANT faces Right. BRIGITTA in front of him.*) All right. You can go, all of you. (*They start to go. Seriously.*) You think me a hard man. Only the priests talk to you of love. (*He puts his hand on BRIGITTA's head and she squirms coyly.*) But this child is worth more to me than the Pope in Rome. (*In a flash of anger.*) Get out, I tell you! (*The CROWD leaves. The LIEUTENANT still has his hand on BRIGITTA's head. There only remain with them MARIA and the PRIEST. The LIEUTENANT turns towards them.*) I told you to go.

MARIA. This is my house.

PRIEST. It's our daughter.

LIEUT. Oh, yes, of course. Your daughter. (PRIEST

goes round to Up Left. LIEUTENANT *is ill at ease with children. He doesn't know how to win* BRIGITTA'S *confidence. He sits down and takes the child on his knees. He speaks to her gently, a little awkwardly.*) You heard what I told them? They are all stupid, the old. The young have to help me. Think again. Haven't you seen any stranger in the village? (BRIGITTA *is silent.*) Somebody you don't know? (*Silence.*)

MARIA. (*Frightened.*) She's stupid. She won't talk to anyone.

LIEUT. (*To* BRIGITTA, *gently.*) You've swallowed your tongue? You don't know how to speak?

MARIA. Lieutenant—

LIEUT. (*Dryly.*) This is my job. Do you think it amuses me to take hostages? To kill people who have done no harm? (*He turns back to* BRIGITTA.) What's your name? (*Silence.*) You don't even know your name? (*A short pause.*) And me? Do you know who I am? (BRIGITTA *for the first time makes a movement. She says "Yes" with her head. The* LIEUTENANT *is surprised.*) So you know me?

BRIGITTA. (*Her only response is to touch his revolver holster.*) That's a gun. (*Kneel.*)

LIEUT. Yes.

BRIGITTA. Let me see it. (*She begins to undo the holster. The* LIEUTENANT *takes the revolver out and shows it to her.*)

LIEUT. It's not for a little girl.

BRIGITTA. It's to kill people. Have you ever killed anyone with it?

LIEUT. No.

BRIGITTA. You'd like to kill someone, wouldn't you? (*The* LIEUTENANT *shows the trigger to* BRIGITTA *who suddenly snatches it from him and pulls it. The revolver is loaded and goes off. The bullet strikes the ground. Quite calmly* BRIGITTA *hands the revolver back to the* LIEUTENANT. *She rubs her shoulder which has been bruised by the recoil of the revolver. She laughs a little.*) It hurt my arm.

(*The* LIEUTENANT *puts back his revolver in the holster. He is watched by* MARIA *and the* PRIEST *who fear his anger, but he is only surprised and intrigued by the child.*)

MARIA. (*Takes her.*) Lieutenant, she is only a child—you must excuse.

(BRIGITTA *goes Down Left.*)

LIEUT. My congratulations. You have a daughter who can defend herself. (*Salutes* BRIGITTA *and he goes out.* MARIA *follows to doorway.*)

PRIEST. I did my best. (*Crosses Center.*) It was their job to give me up. I can't do that.

MARIA. (*Right.*) He took the best man in the village.

PRIEST. Twelve men have been shot because of me. But what can I do if they won't betray me? I look into every face and hope—he may be the one. He never is. He only dies for me and leaves me here. Give me my case. I'm going. I will be as careful as I can. (*She gives him the case from its hiding place behind cupboard.*) And the wine, Maria. It's, the last bottle I have. (MARIA *takes the bottle out of laundry basket, but she doesn't give it to him.*) There's enough for twelve more Masses.

MARIA. (*Up Center, whipping up her anger.*) Masses? Do you think God wants you to stay and die—a whiskey priest like you? Suppose you die. You'll be a martyr, won't you? What kind of a martyr do you think you'll be? That's what makes people laugh at the Church.

PRIEST. Give me the wine and I'll go.

(MARIA *suddenly takes cork off the bottle and holds the bottle downwards while the* PRIEST *watches the wine drain away into bucket Down Right.* BRIGITTA *goes to Right of table.*)

MARIA. You've said your last Mass. Even if it brings a curse on me—

PRIEST. You mustn't be superstitious. It was only wine. There's nothing sacred in wine. It's hard to buy, that's all. (*Takes empty bottle and puts it on cupboard.*) Brigitta. (*He advances shyly. Kneels Right of her.*) Good-bye, Brigitta. (*The* CHILD *waits for him. He kneels down beside her.*) Listen to me. Try to understand. I am your father and I love you. You are so—so important. The Governor up in the city goes guarded by men with guns, but you have all the angels . . .

(*The* CHILD *suddenly spits in his face, giggles and goes out of doorway. He crosses the back and exits Left. The* CHILD *continues to giggle.*)

CURTAIN

ACT II

SCENE FIVE

The MESTIZO *sits on the pavement edge Left Center in
front of the Drop Curtain. He has taken off his shirt
and is examining the seams. The* PRIEST *enters and
passes him. The* MESTIZO *looks up. When the* PRIEST
goes Down Right the MESTIZO *speaks.*

MESTIZO. You're a stranger. (*The* PRIEST *pauses.*)
Have you come from the country?

PRIEST. Yes.

MESTIZO. Are you looking for someone? (*The* PRIEST
makes a vague gesture.) I'm a city man myself. I know
everyone here. From the Governor downwards. (*He nips
a bug in the seams and crushes it between his nails. With
a sigh of satisfaction he puts on his shirt again.*) Looking
for a whore-house? I know the best.

PRIEST. No. (*Comes to Right of* MESTIZO.)

MESTIZO. Sit down. The pavement's free. What are you
afraid of? Are the police looking for you? I know a good
hide-out.

PRIEST. No.

MESTIZO. (*Feels the cloth of the* PRIEST'S *trousers.*)
How much did they cost?

PRIEST. They were given me.

MESTIZO. Given? Why do you lie to me? People don't
give things—except to the rich.

PRIEST. All the same a poor man gave them to me.
(*Hat off.*)

MESTIZO. Sit down, can't you, you make me uneasy
standing there like a statue. (*He giggles.*) A holy statue.

PRIEST. (*Sits down on the pavement beside him.*) Not
very holy.

MESTIZO. I've always had to slave—for a bare crust.

34

Sometimes I feel I would do anything—anything—for a few pesos. Can you blame me?

PRIEST. No. Why should I?

MESTIZO. Would it be wrong if I got a man by the throat, on a dark night like this, and squeezed a few pesos . . . (*Hands round his throat.*)

PRIEST. It wouldn't be worth the risk in my case. I've exactly twenty-nine pesos in the world. I haven't eaten myself for forty-eight hours.

MESTIZO. Mother of God. Why do you lie to me all the time? Lying's a sin.

PRIEST. I'm not lying.

MESTIZO. Then why haven't you eaten—if you've got twenty-nine pesos?

PRIEST. I want to spend them on drink.

MESTIZO. What sort of drink?

PRIEST. The kind of drink a stranger doesn't know how to get.

MESTIZO. You mean spirits?

PRIEST. Yes—and wine.

MESTIZO. How much would you pay? For an introduction to someone who could let you have brandy—real fine Vera Cruz brandy.

PRIEST. With a throat like this, it's wine I really want.

MESTIZO. Pulque, mescal—he's got everything.

PRIEST. Wine? (*Rises.*)

MESTIZO. Quince wine. (*Rises.*)

PRIEST. I'd give you fifteen pesos for some really genuine grape wine.

MESTIZO. Come with me. (*Going Right.*) It's your lucky day, all right, meeting the right man, just like this, at a street corner. Do you believe in guidance? (*They exit Right.*)

BLACKOUT

SCENE SIX

A hotel bedroom. An iron bed, a bare electric globe, a plain table, one or two basket chairs.

LIFT comes up. The door opens and the MESTIZO *enters. He switches on the LIGHT. The* PRIEST *follows.*

MESTIZO. We'll wait for him here. (*Goes to table Left Center.*)

PRIEST. (*Right.*) You're sure he can get it?

MESTIZO. He can get anything. You know why? He's the Governor's cousin. He gets it from the Customs.

PRIEST. (*Crosses Left Center. After a restless pause.*) How much longer will he be?

MESTIZO. Give him a chance! He's a busy man— knows all the high-up people. You know who's his friend? The Chief of Police. He runs this hotel, but that's only a sideline of his—

PRIEST. You're quite sure—that he—?

MESTIZO. I've told you, haven't I? (PRIEST *walks to and fro Left.*) What's the matter with you? Sit down. (PRIEST *sits Left.*) I don't ask any questions. You promised me fifteen pesos if I'd get you a drink. Now you've put me to the trouble— (*Left of bed, picks up tie.*)

PRIEST. (*Rises.*) It wasn't—just drink. I said wine. (*Crosses to him.*)

MESTIZO. All right—wine.

PRIEST. Wine or *nothing.*

MESTIZO. I heard you—wine.

PRIEST. Not homemade wine—French wine.

MESTIZO. Californian?

PRIEST. That would do.

MESTIZO. You look to me like a man who'd drink anything.

PRIEST. (*Takes some money from his pocket and begins to count it.*) I'll give you fifteen pesos. Then you can buy the wine for me, and keep the change. (*Gives him money.*)

MESTIZO. (*Goes Left and looks in mirror.*) They don't like dealing with someone they don't know. And you— (*He laughs.*) You look like—I don't know what. But as long as you're with me you're all right.

PRIEST. What do I look like then?

MESTIZO. A man with a thirst, eh? (*He laughs and takes the money. The LIGHT flickers and goes out.*) If it's not the city it's the hotel, and if it's not the hotel it's the city. We should have gone to the movies. For once in my life I've got a bit of money, and there's no light to see it with. (*The LIGHT flickers and comes on.*) Ah! Not so bad this time. (*He goes to light Down Right.*) Last night it was off for an hour. (*He counts the coins lovingly.*)

PRIEST. (*Watching him.*) Are you so fond of money? (*Crosses Center.*)

MESTIZO. Everyone is—when they haven't got any. Like me. . . .

PRIEST. I understand.

MESTIZO. No. If you've got fifteen pesos to spend on drink, you can't understand. (*Sound of a LIFT. Takes tie off, puts it in pocket.*) That sounds like him. If you get your wine, you won't forget to offer him a glass? It pays to be polite to the Governor's cousin.

PRIEST. (*Left Center.*) But I wasn't going to open it here. I wanted to take it away . . .

MESTIZO. (*Center.*) Where to?

PRIEST. Home. (*LIFT comes up.*)

MESTIZO. You know where home is? Any place where there's two glasses and a table!

(*He laughs. The LIGHT dims and goes out. The MESTIZO curses. A stumble and a curse. GOVERNOR'S COUSIN enters. The LIGHT comes on again.*)

COUSIN. On and off, on and off—it's like— Oh, it's you. Who's this? (*Crosses Center.*)

MESTIZO. A friend of mine. Wants to talk to you.

COUSIN. (*Mistrustful.*) What about?

MESTIZO. He's got a thirst.

COUSIN. There's water in the tap. And beer downstairs. (*Looks at ceiling fan. Puts chair under it.*)

MESTIZO. He doesn't want beer.

COUSIN. (*Studying the* PRIEST.) What does he want? Brandy?

PRIEST. No, Excellency.

COUSIN. Well, what then? (*Takes magazine from bed, stands on chair and taps fan. It starts.*)

PRIEST. Wine—Excellency.

COUSIN. Wine? Don't you know it's against the law?

PRIEST. I'm aware of that, Excellency, but— (*Off chair.*)

COUSIN. He's "aware" of it, eh? Ha! You talk like a priest.

PRIEST. If you can't help me—I'm sorry I've troubled you—

COUSIN. (*To him.*) You've come in here to ask me to break the law?

PRIEST. Yes, Excellency.

(MESTIZO *puts chair back.*)

COUSIN. That makes you a criminal.

PRIEST. Yes, Excellency.

COUSIN. I could have you arrested.

PRIEST. Yes, Excellency.

COUSIN. I'm a patriot. I won't break the laws of my country.

PRIEST. Of course—

COUSIN. If I happen to have—any of the stuff you want, it's only because it was given to me. Legally, you understand? Confiscated by the Customs.

MESTIZO. That's what I told him.

COUSIN. And to keep things legal costs money.

PRIEST. I gave some to him. (*The* MESTIZO *jingles the coins Left Center.*)

COUSIN. All right. (*He rummages in the mattress of the bed.*) Can you keep your mouth shut? (*Left of it.*)

PRIEST. (*Right of it.*) I know how to keep a secret, Excellency.

COUSIN. (*Pulling out a bottle.*) There you are. Good stuff. Real Vera Cruz brandy. (*Gives it to him.*)

PRIEST. But—it was wine I asked for. (*Gives it back.*)

COUSIN. I haven't wine. You must take what comes.

PRIEST. I see. It doesn't matter. (*Crosses to the* MESTIZO.) Will you give me back my fifteen pesos?

COUSIN. Fifteen pesos? (*The* MESTIZO *nods.*) Oh—that's different. For fifteen pesos I can let you have two bottles. How's that? It's the best Vera Cruz brandy.

PRIEST. Oh, I'm sure of it. But, Excellency, I only want wine. Could you make it one bottle of brandy and one of wine?

COUSIN. Wine costs more. How much can you pay?

PRIEST. Another ten pesos?

COUSIN. Twenty-five for the two?

PRIEST. (*Eagerly.*) Yes. But real wine, Excellency—

COUSIN. (*Puts brandy on table.*) What do you take me for? (*Crosses Down Left to cane chair. The* PRIEST *gives money to* MESTIZO. *The* COUSIN *rummages in the cane chair. He produces the bottle. The* PRIEST *looks at the label. He is overjoyed. The* COUSIN *gives the two bottles to* PRIEST.) You see? I always do my best to give my customers satisfaction. (MESTIZO *gives money to* COUSIN.)

PRIEST. I'm most—grateful, Excellency. (*Goes Right with the bottles.*)

COUSIN. (*Left Center.*) Aren't you thirsty?

(*The* MESTIZO, *Center, signals the* PRIEST.)

PRIEST. (*Right.*) Would your Excellency do me the honor—?

COUSIN. Why not? (*Sits Left of table. He signals to the* MESTIZO, *who collects some tooth glasses from bathroom, as from habit. Stretching himself in a chair.*) That damned Government beer downstairs—it gives me gripe.

PRIEST. (*Right of table.*) A glass of brandy, Excellency? (MESTIZO *puts glasses on table.*)

COUSIN. Can't stand the stuff. Now, a glass of wine—that's good for the blood. Iron.

PRIEST. If you don't mind—I was keeping the wine for a present— (*He begins hastily to open the brandy, but the* MESTIZO *takes the bottle of wine from him.*)

COUSIN. All the better. You'll have tried it first. (*The* MESTIZO *opens wine, serves the* COUSIN. *Goes to pour for* PRIEST.) Guests come first.

PRIEST. Thank you—I'd rather have brandy. (*He pours himself a glass of brandy, and watches anxiously as the* MESTIZO *fills two generous glasses of wine for himself and the* COUSIN.)

COUSIN. (*Sampling the wine.*) Hm . . . though I say it myself, it's not too bad. Chairs, you fool. (MESTIZO *fetches chairs—one back of table, one Left.*)

PRIEST. (*Drinks his brandy at a gulp. It makes him feel better.*) I beg your pardon, Excellency. Your health! (*He swallows the last drop.*)

COUSIN. Health. . . . (*He drinks.*)

PRIEST. The brandy's very good. Will you—? (*He offers the bottle.*)

COUSIN. Of course it's good. If you like brandy. But I'll keep to the wine. (*He holds out his glass. The* PRIEST *has to fill it. The* MESTIZO *holds out his glass too.*)

PRIEST. No. I told you—I want to keep some—for a present. (*He corks the wine bottle. Sits back of table. Puts wine under table.*)

COUSIN. Who for? A girl?

PRIEST. For my mother. (*He pours himself more brandy.*)

COUSIN. She knows what's good for her. Drink wine, and you'll never have boils. Did you know that?

PRIEST. No, Excellency.

COUSIN. It's fact. When I was shaving this morning, I felt the first sign of a boil just coming round here. . . . (*He touches his neck and eyes the bottle.*) So I think I'll have a little more medicine. (*The* PRIEST *tries to ignore the* COUSIN'S *glance, then he has to give in. He fills it, puts bottle on chair behind him.*) So your mother's still alive?

PRIEST. Yes.

COUSIN. Where does she live?

PRIEST. (*Inventing quickly.*) Yucatan.

COUSIN. Mine's in Mexico City, so I don't see much of her. All the same, it's good to have someone—you know what I mean?

PRIEST. Yes—it's good to have someone.

COUSIN. And a mother means more than a father. (*He empties his glass. Puts it on table. He reaches for the wine bottle. The* PRIEST *tries to take it, but the* MESTIZO *is too quick for him; he snatches the bottle and pours out full glass for the* COUSIN. *The* PRIEST *grabs back the bottle and puts it on the table. Indignantly, to the* MESTIZO.) Is that *your* wine? Where are your manners? My friend, I insist. (*He takes the bottle and tries to pour some for the* PRIEST, *who refuses.*)

PRIEST. No. No, thank you—your brandy is so good. (*He pours himself a glass and drinks.*)

COUSIN. What was I saying? Yes—mothers. . . . A mother means more than a father—you can't deny it. Now my mother— (*Rises, goes Right.*) I can honestly say, without fear of contradiction, that my mother is an angel. Of course, nowadays, angels are illegal, but you know what I mean. . . . (*He puts on GRAMOPHONE up Right Center, stretches himself on the bed. The* PRIEST *sees his chance. He begins to stuff the bottle in his pocket.*)

MESTIZO. (*Soulfully.*) I had a mother—once.

COUSIN. No one asked you to talk!

(PRIEST *goes below table to Right.*)

MESTIZO. I was talking to myself—

COUSIN. You're drunk!

(*A NOISE on the stairs.*)

VOICE. (*Off.*) Anyone in?

MESTIZO. It's the Chief of Police. (PRIEST *tries to hide bottles.*) Don't worry, he's all right.

COUSIN. Is that you, Chief?

VOICE. (*Off.*) Who the devil do you think it is?

COUSIN. We've company! (*The* CHIEF OF POLICE *enters Right. He is in a very bad temper.*) Have a good game of billiards?

CHIEF. No.

COUSIN. Beaten?

CHIEF. Yes. By that damned dentist. (*To table. The* MESTIZO *puts a fourth glass on the table.*) Oh . . .

COUSIN. This is—a friend.

CHIEF. (*Looking at the* PRIEST.) Where have I seen you before?

PRIEST. Never—so far as I know—Excellency.

CHIEF. What are you doing up here? (*Picks up glass, smells.*) Ah!

COUSIN. Have a drink with us?

CHIEF. Mm . . . a glass of beer never did anyone any harm. (*Sits above table.*)

(*They laugh.*)

COUSIN. (*To the* MESTIZO.) A glass of beer for the Chief. (*He takes brandy from* PRIEST.) I said a glass of beer for the Chief. (*The* MESTIZO *puts his hand out to the* PRIEST. *The* PRIEST *has to give him the wine. The* MESTIZO *fills a glass.*) Don't juggle with it. The Chief can remember when wine-drinking was an art.

CHIEF. (*Tastes it.* ALL *await his verdict.*) I don't know why this damn' Government beer's always so confoundedly flat. (*They laugh. The* PRIEST *tries to smile. The* CHIEF *empties his glass and takes the wine bottle from the* PRIEST. *It is three-quarters empty.*) Is that all you've got?

COUSIN. Beer's getting scarce.

CHIEF. Mustn't waste it, then. (*He fills his glass: to*

the PRIEST.) Some for you? (*The* PRIEST *can only shake his head.*) Aren't you drinking?

PRIEST. I would rather have brandy. (*He fills himself a glass.* CHIEF *pours himself wine.*)

CHIEF. (*Rises.*) Good health. (*Steps to Center.*)

PRIEST. Good health, your Excellency.

COUSIN. (*As the* CHIEF *looks at him with raised eyebrows.*) Oh, he calls everyone "excellency."

CHIEF. Fault on the right side, I suppose. Well, don't let me spoil your party. What were you talking about?

(PRIEST *sits Left of table.*)

COUSIN. (*Getting a little maudlin.*) Mothers—I was just saying that mine's an angel.

CHIEF. Mine's underneath one.

COUSIN. Underneath what?

CHIEF. An angel. Italian marble. Cost me four thousand pesos. Every anniversary I take a wreath. I've missed her, you know, since she went. Say what you like, a mother's a necessity.

COUSIN. Doctors would agree. (*They laugh.*)

MESTIZO. (*In a silence.*) I can remember my grandmother.

COUSIN. What color was she? (*Lies back on bed, feet on rail.*)

CHIEF. Let him be. Don't we all have our memories? I remember my first Communion. Shouldn't say it, of course, but they can't make a law against remembering. And the priest. An old man. His hands shook when he held the—what d'you call it? (CHIEF *down to table.*)

PRIEST. Chalice.

CHIEF. Now he's dead. Shot last year. Perhaps he's in heaven—then he'll pray for me. I had a photograph of myself, all dressed up for the procession. Me, and my sister in her veil, standing in the garden surrounded by my parents. (*Takes hold of wine bottle.*)

COUSIN. How many did you have?

CHIEF. What?

COUSIN. Parents.

CHIEF. Two. What d'you mean?

COUSIN. You said "surrounded."

CHIEF. Oh! (*They laugh. A silence. Distant THUN-DER. The* CHIEF *has the wine bottle and empties it into his glass. He holds it upside down, letting the last drop run out.* PRIEST, *rising, takes bottle from him.*) Oh, sorry. It's your beer, isn't it?

(COUSIN *goes into bathroom.*)

PRIEST. It doesn't matter—Excellency.

CHIEF. (*Looks at the* PRIEST *closely.*) What are you crying for?

PRIEST. (*Choked with tears.*) Nothing—nothing—it's the brandy—I'm not used to it. (*He pulls himself together, tries to seem gay.*) It's—beer, I'm used to.

CHIEF. (*Still watches the* PRIEST, *unable to understand.*) I offered you some. You wouldn't take it.

PRIEST. I was leaving it for you, Excellency. I shouldn't have refused, I—I want beer, beer. Couldn't I have another bottle? (*Rising—goes round table to Up Center.*)

COUSIN. (*Re-enters from bathroom Up Center.*) Have you got the money?

PRIEST. Yes. . . . (*Another rumble of THUNDER. The* COUSIN *goes mistrustfully to the cane chair and takes out another bottle of wine. The* CHIEF *is still looking suspiciously at the* PRIEST.) It will be the same sort of—beer, won't it? I don't want—(*He touches the brandy bottle.*)—mineral water. (COUSIN *hands wine to* CHIEF *who gives it to* PRIEST. COUSIN *snatches it, opens it and pours some into own glass. Suddenly,* PRIEST *sits. The strain and the drink have been too much for him. He wipes his eyes. He is conscious that the others are watching him.*) Some sorts of drink always seem to run out of one's eyes—I've known it happen before—and then—I start to see things.

CHIEF. What things?

PRIEST. I see—all the hope of the world—draining away.

COUSIN. Man, you're a poet. (*To above Right of him.*)

CHIEF. (*Rise to Left of* PRIEST. *Gives him his glass.*) A poet is the soul of his country. I could swear I've seen you before.

PRIEST. I haven't had the honor. (COUSIN *puts on* GRAMOPHONE.)

CHIEF. That's another mystery. The way you think you've seen people before—and places. Was it in a dream or in a past life? Do you believe in reincarnation?

(MESTIZO *sits Left of table.*)

COUSIN. Sometimes—in front of my glass—I think to myself perhaps in the old days I was Cardinal of Mexico. I have the presence. (*He raises his hand in blessing and then laughs.*) That's when I learned to appreciate good wine.

(PRIEST *kneels by table—picks up full wine bottle.*)

CHIEF. I think perhaps I was a great actor. Romeo . . . perhaps not.

MESTIZO. Who was Romeo?

COUSIN. Shut up. (*To above table.*) You've been re-incarnated as a pimp. Now you, sir, you're a poet. You know what it means to feel greatness inside you and be surrounded by circumstances of extreme squalor. (*Picks up brandy bottle.* PRIEST *rises.*)

CHIEF. Squalor?

COUSIN. Squalor! My cousin, the governor, turns a cold shoulder. You, sir, remind me of him. You stand there silent while I pour out my soul to you.

CHIEF. (*Up Right of* PRIEST, *raising glass to* PRIEST.) His Excellency.

COUSIN. Your Excellency. Come off your pedestal, your Excellency, and mingle with the common men. (*Grabs* PRIEST *and forces him Up Left Center.*)

CHIEF. Not common. (*Takes bottle from him.*)

COUSIN. I stand corrected. (*To* MESTIZO.) Why are you grinning, fool?

MESTIZO. Him an Excellency.

COUSIN. (*Picks up empty wine bottle.*) If I say he's an Excellency, he is an Excellency. Drink to him, fool. (CHIEF *takes bottle from him.* COUSIN *to Down Right below bed.*) Drink to him, my oldest and dearest friend. Excellency of Excellencies. True God of True God. You haven't paid me.

(*The LIGHTS go off.*)

CHIEF. When will they get this confounded electricity to work?

(*The LIGHTS come on. The* PRIEST *has gone.* COUSIN *sits bed—looks round.*)

COUSIN. (*Rises.*) Where is he? Stop him! Thief! (*To corridor opening.*)

MESTIZO. (*Running out.*) Stop, thief! Thief! (*Exits opening in corridor.*)

COUSIN. He never paid me. (*Crosses below bed to gramophone.*)

CHIEF. (*Up Left.*) Nice friends you ask me to drink with.

COUSIN. And what's more—he's enough of a fool to get caught with it. (*Turns off GRAMOPHONE, picks up record.*)

CHIEF. That's his lookout. (*A POLICE WHISTLE in the street. They run to the window. The* CHIEF *leans out.*) They're round the corner. (*Both to Left Center.*)

COUSIN. The Governor's given instructions to double the penalties. And your lieutenant's got fancy ideas of doing his duty. Suppose he talks?

CHIEF. (*Crosses Right Center, putting on cap.*) I'll talk first. You'd better come and give me moral support.

COUSIN. No, no—I'll keep out of it. I'll lose my license.

CHIEF. (*Steps to him, firmly.*) We may need influence. From your cousin the Governor—come on! (*Crosses Right and exits corridor opening.*)

COUSIN. (*Smashing gramophone record on the rail of the bed.*) This *would* happen! Just when I've organized a reliable supply— (*Follows him off.*)

BLACKOUT

SCENE SEVEN

Street Scene

The PRIEST *runs on, from Right, hugging the bottle in his coat. He sees a* REDSHIRT *and turns back, to find the redshirt* CORPORAL *behind him. They close in on either side of him in silence.*

CORPORAL. In a hurry?
REDSHIRT. Where have you come from?

(MESTIZO *enters Down Right. Stands Downstage.*)

PRIEST. A friend's house.
REDSHIRT. What have you got under your coat?
PRIEST. (*Center.*) A bottle of—mineral water.
CORPORAL. (*Left.*) Is that what you've been drinking?
PRIEST. I take it at night—with my quinine.
REDSHIRT. (*Right.*) He stinks worse than the harbour wall.
CORPORAL. Let's see the bottle.
CHIEF'S VOICE. (*Off.*) Corporal! (CHIEF *enters, followed by* COUSIN.)
CORPORAL. (*Coming to attention.*) Sir.
CHIEF. Ah! I'm glad you've caught the fellow. He was making a row in the street outside the hotel. Drunk. Disturbing the clients. Have you searched him?

CORPORAL. He's got a bottle, sir.

CHIEF. (*Crosses, pulls the bottle from the* PRIEST'S *coat.*) Wine— Now where would you have got this?

CORPORAL. Answer!

CHIEF. No. They're all alike, these cases. You can never get anything out of them. Not a thing. Shut him up in the jail tonight, and in the morning I'll consider how to deal with him. (*Both* POLICEMEN *cross Left with* PRIEST.)

CORPORAL. (*Over his shoulder.*) The Lieutenant gave orders—

CHIEF. I am not the Lieutenant. Nor is the Lieutenant Chief of Police. Take him to the jail. (*The* PRIEST *is led off Down Left.*)

COUSIN. (*Right Center.*) Suppose he talks—in the jail?

CHIEF. (*Center.*) It's a risk we've got to take.

COUSIN. (*Turning on the* MESTIZO *who has come to his Right.*) You! You're the cause of this! Bringing that fool in.

MESTIZO. I could see he didn't talk, Excellency.

COUSIN. Get to your bug-ridden bed if you've got one—

MESTIZO. I know the warder at the jail. I could go inside. And if he talks—there are ways. You can fix things in the jail.

CHIEF. He's right. Go on, then.

MESTIZO. (*Crosses to Left of* CHIEF.) I'll need money, Excellencies.

COUSIN. You got your commission for bringing that fool to the hotel.

MESTIZO. But the warder—

COUSIN. (*Giving him a coin after seeing the* CHIEF *is unlikely to oblige.*) There you are. Hurry.

MESTIZO. (*Looking at the coin reproachfully—going.*) It's less than I get for holding a mule. (*Exits Left.*)

COUSIN. You can't trust a soul these days. (*He looks at the wine bottle the* CHIEF *is still holding—he takes the bottle.*) Not a soul. (*Exits Right followed by the* CHIEF.)

BLACKOUT

SCENE EIGHT

The Prison. The small hours of the morning

*A common cell, in which young and old, male and female,
guilty and innocent are confined together. Some are
in rags, some in dirty drill suits, some in peasants'
clothes. One or two have bundles of possessions.*

*To the Left, an opening, which leads to the yard. Along
the back of the cell an iron grille with a locked gate.
Through the grille a passage. In the passage a desk
with a register, and a feeble light. In the cell, beside
the grille, a urine bucket. SNORES, COUGHS,
SPITTING, MUMBLES. Somewhere from outside,
a KNOCKING on the gate of the jail.*

SPINSTER. (*Calling.*) Warder!

A DRUNKARD. (*Suddenly sitting up in a shaft of
LIGHT.*) Caterina! Caterina! Caterina!

PRISONER. (*Sitting up.*) For the hundredth time it's
not Caterina.

(*A man called LOPEZ rises to stretch himself.*)

SPINSTER. Warder!

LOPEZ. Who is Caterina? His wife?

PRISONER. His daughter. Can't you sleep, Grandfather?

SPINSTER. Warder!

DRUNKARD. It's the priests—they turned her against
me. It's all the fault of the priests. (*Lies down.*)

SPINSTER. Quite right, too. A fine father he'd make.
(*The* SPINSTER *arranges herself primly. She is middle-
aged and aggressively respectable.*)

LOPEZ. If you're so virtuous, why are you in here?

(WARDER *enters Right. Behind grille.*)

SPINSTER. They searched my house and found Holy books. Warder! I wish to complain. I insist on being transferred to another cell. (*Stepping from Up Left towards gate Right Center.*)

WARDER. What d'you think this is—a hotel? (*Outside gate Right Center.*)

SPINSTER. I shouldn't have been put in here in the first place.

VOICE. Get out, then.

SPINSTER. I should be in the women's cell—

WARDER. We haven't got one.

SPINSTER. Oh, yes, you have! I know you have!

WARDER. How d'you know? Have you been here before?

(*TITTERS in the darkness.*)

SPINSTER. I came here some years ago—when I was engaged on social work. I visited female prisoners and they were kept in a separate cell.

WARDER. Well, we haven't another cell now, d'you hear me? The one you mean's been taken over for offices—

SPINSTER. I don't believe it.

WARDER. What are you grumbling about? It's dark and there's plenty of men. Go on and enjoy yourself. (*Goes Up Left.*)

(*Ribald LAUGHTER. SPINSTER is pushed about and she gets Down Center.*)

SPINSTER. That's exactly what I'm complaining about. Over there in the corner—those two—if you only *knew* what's going on! (*LAUGHTER from a dark corner, Down Left, where a GIRL and a MAN are intertwined.*)

GIRL'S VOICE. Just listen to her! She's jealous! (*A roar of LAUGHTER.*)

SPINSTER. It's disgusting—disgraceful! (*Climbing over*

bodies to Up Left.) I warn you! I shall complain to the Lieutenant. (*Sits on her bundle.*)

VOICES. Oh, tell the old bitch to keep her mouth shut! Let's get some sleep! Put her outside!

WARDER. (*Left side of grille.*) Quiet, the lot of you! Quiet, I said! (*Silence. The* PRISONERS *settle themselves, grumbling.*) If I hear any more noise, I'll be using this. (*Takes out revolver.*)

LOPEZ. Oh, go on, use it then. (WARDER *taps his holster and moves away down the passage Right. He admits the two* POLICEMEN *with the sobbing* PRIEST.) He'll use his gun! He's never shot anything bigger than a rabbit.

DRUNKARD. Caterina . . .

(*The LIGHT is growing. The* WARDER *comes down the passage with the* PRIEST *and the* POLICEMEN. *He opens the register.*)

WARDER. Name? (*At table back Center.*)

PRIEST. Montez.

WARDER. Charge?

POLICEMAN. He had wine.

WARDER. (*Writing.*) "In possession of alcohol." . . . Got it from a stranger, I suppose? (*Rises, unlocks gate.*)

PRIEST. Yes.

WARDER. Whom you can't identify?

PRIEST. No.

WARDER. That's the way.

PRIEST. Could I have a drink of water?

WARDER. (*He has now unlocked the gate in the grille.*) It isn't long till breakfast—you can wait till then. (*The gate jams against a prisoner. It is* LOPEZ.) You—you there! Get out of the way!

LOPEZ. (*With a yelp.*) Look where you're going, can't you?

WARDER. D'you know who you're talking to?

LOPEZ. Yes, I don't care—there's no need to kick me in the guts! (*He shifts, muttering.*)

WARDER. Come on! Make room, will you! (*He locks*

the gate behind the PRIEST, *exchanges words with the* POLICEMEN *and then sees them to the gate. They exit.*)

LOPEZ. First time?

PRIEST. Yes. (*Standing Up Left.*)

LOPEZ. Any cigarettes?

PRIEST. No.

LOPEZ. Any money?

PRIEST. No. I'm sorry. (*He tries to find room to lie down.*)

A VOICE. Look out, can't you?

(*The* PRIEST *stumbles against the urine bucket. A* MAN *sits up, furious.*)

PRISONER. Get away from the bucket! D'you want to drown us?

PRIEST. I'm sorry. Is it water?

PRISONER. Are you thirsty?

PRIEST. Yes.

PRISONER. Try it. (*A SNIGGER in the dark.*) Got anything to eat?

PRIEST. No.

PRISONER. Then lie down and keep quiet.

PRIEST. If you could move a little—

PRISONER. No one moves for anyone in here. Last come, last served. (*But some of the others make space and the* SPINSTER *is jostled.*)

SPINSTER. Keep away from me!

LOPEZ. Move over against the wall.

(PRIEST *sits Center.*)

SPINSTER. Don't push me! It's disgraceful! I'll complain—

LOPEZ. (*Menacing.*) I've heard enough of you! You keep your mouth shut.

SPINSTER. (*Rises.*) Do you think I'll take orders from you? Killer! (LOPEZ *springs at her. She goes on screaming. They hold* LOPEZ *back.*) Killer—killer—killer! (*The*

PRIEST *separates them. No one else takes any action, except to jeer or protest.*)

LOPEZ. You heard what she called me?

PRIEST. She didn't mean it.

SPINSTER. It's true! You ask him!

PRIEST. Is it true?

LOPEZ. Yes—I killed him. (*A pause. The* SPINSTER *and the* PRIEST *sit down again. Moving Down Right and sitting.*) He called my mother a whore. My mother——

PRIEST. So you killed him?

LOPEZ. I pushed a bottle in his face. How did I know he'd die? And after what he called my mother—you don't call it murder, do you, when it's done for honor?

PRIEST. It's a terrible thing—to kill a man.

DRUNKARD. (*Rising.*) Priests—all the fault of the priests——

PRIEST. (*Puts him down again.*) What is the fault of the priests?

LOPEZ. They took his daughter. Put her in a convent.

SPINSTER. The child was a bastard. They acted correctly.

PRIEST. A bastard— It's not a nice name to give a child. . . . Why did they take her away from him?

SPINSTER. (*Rising, slowly to Left of* PRIEST, *sits.*) Because he drinks. She was safer in the convent. And just to show you how right they were—when the priests were driven out, she wouldn't go back to him.

PRIEST. Why not?

SPINSTER. Because the Priests had taught her properly.

PRIEST. Where is she now?

LOPEZ. (*Matter-of-fact.*) In a brothel.

SPINSTER. And whose fault is that? The children pay for the sins of the fathers.

PRIEST. But—they shouldn't have done it. A child should love her father. They had no right to touch that.

SPINSTER. A father like him?

PRIEST. Her father.

SPINSTER. The priests know what they're doing.

PRIEST. Not all of them.

SPINSTER. They can judge better than you.

PRIEST. But . . . I am a priest.

(*Absolute silence. FIGURES rise on one elbow. Whispers: "Priest '. . . says he's a priest . . ." Then silence again.*)

LOPEZ. Is that why you're here?

PRIEST. No. They haven't found out. Not yet—

SPINSTER. You shouldn't have said it, Father. There are all sorts here—thieves, murderers—

LOPEZ. (*Kneeling up.*) Just because I've killed a man, it doesn't mean I'd do that. We are honest people here—except you.

SPINSTER. They'll shoot you, Father.

(*They* ALL *group a little towards him.*)

PRIEST. Yes.

A VOICE. Are you afraid?

PRIEST. Of course.

A VOICE. It doesn't hurt—all over in a second.

PRIEST. (*Looking towards the voice.*) All the same, I am afraid. We can't all be brave men.

LOPEZ. They haven't recognized you yet.

PRIEST. No. But there's a reward of seven hundred pesos. (*Reaction; they draw back.*)

SPINSTER. Are you mad? Why do you tell them that?

PRISONERS. (*Furious with her, shout together.*) What do you think we are? Just because we're in prison . . . If you weren't a woman . . . (*The* SPINSTER *shrinks back Down Left.*)

LOPEZ. (*Right of him—kneels.*) Anyone would think you wanted us to tell them. (PRIEST *shrugs.*) That's suicide, isn't it? (*A MURMUR of agreement.*) Even if you're the last priest in the country, it's still your duty to do your job. After all most of us here have dangerous jobs.

(A pause. Imperceptibly the PRIEST *has become the center of a group. All eyes upon him.)*

SPINSTER. Father—

PRIEST. Yes?

SPINSTER. I'd like to make—my confession.

PRIEST. Here?

A VOICE. What's she got to confess?

ANOTHER. Evil thoughts? *(A TITTER, but subdued.)*

LOPEZ. Go in a corner. We won't listen.

PRIEST. *(After a pause of indecision.)* Say an act of contrition. God will forgive you. For me all that is over.

SPINSTER. So long as people need you, it's your duty to serve them.

PRIEST. In all this year I said three Masses and heard twenty confessions—

SPINSTER. That's better than nothing.

PRIEST. Twelve men have been shot because of me. I'm supposed to help people and instead I may have damned them. Now I haven't even the wine to say Mass.

SPINSTER. You don't need wine to hear a confession.

PRIEST. Would you want me to hear it? You've a name for me. A whiskey priest. *(Rises to Up Center.)*

SPINSTER. It's not so important. I knew a bishop once—

PRIEST. Don't try and comfort me. Comfort's my job. It's not only spirits I've been drunk with, I have a daughter.

SPINSTER. *(After a pause.)* A daughter?

PRIEST. Yes, a daughter. A bastard like that old man's.

LOPEZ. *(With an uneasy laugh.)* There's always repentance, Father. You tell us that.

PRIEST. I can't repent. I'm not sorry. I love her too much.

SPINSTER. So that's why you spoke up for that old lecher? Oh, it's ugly.

PRIEST. I'm a bad priest, you see. I know—from experience—how much beauty Satan carried down with him when he fell. Nobody ever said the fallen angels were the ugly ones. (*He holds the bars of the gate, Up Center, looking out with longing into the growing daylight. A pause.*)

SPINSTER. Now I can see the sort of priest you are. If your Bishop could hear you—

PRIEST. He's a very long way off.

SPINSTER. And you are the only priest we have left.

(*It is quite light now and the* PRISONERS *turn away from the* PRIEST. *A feeling of disappointment. He finds himself alone, unregarded. One or two* PRISONERS *roll over to sleep. Suddenly the* PRIEST *looks up wildly round the cell.*)

PRIEST. Seven hundred pesos! Seven hundred pesos! Don't you want money? You steal for it, you kill for it! Seven hundred pesos! Will no one be my Judas? (*Comes down—sits Down Center.*)

(*No one moves. No one even looks at him. STEPS in the passage. Enter the* WARDER.)

WARDER. (*With bucket.*) Come on! Get up! (*The* PRISONERS *begin to rise.*) What's the matter with you? (*He kicks the* DRUNKARD.) Come on—you too! (*He opens the door to the yard.*) Outside, all of you—get moving! And start work without being told. (*The* PRISONERS *begin to file out Right into the yard, passing the* WARDER *one by one.*)

SPINSTER. Warder! I wish to speak to the Lieutenant.

WARDER. Get outside with the rest! You can see him when he does his rounds. (*The* SPINSTER *follows the other* PRISONERS.) Here—not you. (*The* PRIEST *is going last. He starts.*) You're privileged this morning. (*Puts bucket down.*) Last in cleans the cell. You can finish by emptying that stinking bucket—down the drain in the yard. (*He goes out.*)

(*The* PRIEST *is alone. He shivers. He goes to the bucket*

and tries to lift it. It is too heavy for him. He does
his best to drag it Up Center. He takes bucket to
Left and washes the floor. Behind the grille the
MESTIZO *enters Right. He watches the* PRIEST
through the bars Right side of grille. He speaks
quietly.)

MESTIZO.   Father . . . (*The* PRIEST *stiffens, but*
doesn't turn round.) Father . . .
PRIEST. (*Turns.*) What are you doing here?
MESTIZO. Can I help you—Father?
PRIEST. Have they arrested you?
MESTIZO. Oh, no. I'm a kind of guest, you might say.
(*Rises.*) You took the last place, so I had to sleep in the
passage. It was a bit draughty. But I could hear. (*To*
door Right Center.)
PRIEST. Hear what? (*On knees.*)
MESTIZO. Everything you said. Through the bars, Fa-
ther. . . .
PRIEST. I see.
MESTIZO. All last night I was wondering—the fuss you
made about the wine. Now I know.
PRIEST. Yes.
MESTIZO. (*To Up Center.*) I'm a good Catholic, Fa-
ther. You won't give yourself up, will you?
PRIEST. You'd rather betray me yourself?
MESTIZO. Some time. Not yet. I like the food here.
There's a roof over your head. And so long as you keep
quiet, the others will too. I know them—they won't
squeal. Father, you will let me have the reward, won't
you?
PRIEST. So I've found you at last. . . . I'm not the
first you've betrayed, am I?
MESTIZO. It's not a betrayal, Father. You said you
wanted—
PRIEST. You followed me here, didn't you? You
planned it. You thought about it at night. It wasn't sudden, was it, like lust?

MESTIZO. (*To Left of grille.*) Lust? I don't know what you are talking about, Father. I don't go after women.

PRIEST. God can forgive a sudden act. Why didn't you give me up in the street? Then was the time.

MESTIZO. I wasn't sure who you were and now I can't. They'd say they've got you already. They'd take the reward for themselves. (*Kneels Left.*) Now if we wait till you're let out, I can follow you, at the right moment. You want to be taken, don't you? And I'm a man who's never had a chance.

PRIEST. (*Suddenly.*) No! (*Down Right Center.*)

MESTIZO. In the name of God. (*He makes a rapid sign of the Cross.*) Forgive me, Father. Just now you were asking them to give you away—

PRIEST. But not by you! By anyone but you!

MESTIZO. Why—? (*Rises.*)

PRIEST. Anyone but you!

MESTIZO. (*In a frenzy—going to Up Right Center.*) What's the matter with you? Why shouldn't I have it? If you tell them—I warn you—if you tell them—! (*Outside door Right Center.*)

(*The* LIEUTENANT *enters from Left to Left of table.*)

LIEUT. What are you shouting for?

MESTIZO. (*Cringing.*) Nothing, Lieutenant.

LIEUT. Get outside, then. (*The* MESTIZO *goes Right. Coming in—the* LIEUTENANT *inspects the cell.*) Is this cell supposed to be cleaned?

PRIEST. Not yet, Lieutenant.

LIEUT. Get on with it, then. (*Goes Left. He inspects the bars, the locks.*)

PRIEST. (*Screws up his courage.*) Lieutenant— (*Rising.*)

LIEUT. Yes? (*A pause: he turns.*) Are you the drunk who came in last night?

PRIEST. (*Left Center.*) Yes, Lieutenant. But . . . (*He tries to speak. He is trembling.*)

LIEUT. Well? What do you want to tell me?

PRIEST. (*A pause. Suddenly puts his hand to his eyes and turns away his head. Weakly, resolution gone.*) I—I wasn't drunk, Lieutenant. I only had wine.

LIEUT. Look at me— Look at me, I said. (*The PRIEST turns. They are face to face.*) Where have I seen you before?

PRIEST. You came to my village, Lieutenant. Santa Maria.

LIEUT. What are you doing in the town?

PRIEST. I came to buy tools, Lieutenant.

LIEUT. And spent the money on drink?

PRIEST. Yes, Lieutenant.

LIEUT. So you've no money to pay your fine?

PRIEST. No, Lieutenant.

LIEUT. What are you going to do?

PRIEST. God knows. (*On to knees—commences cleaning again.*)

LIEUT. God knows, God knows! You're all alike, you peasants! When will you learn the truth—that God knows nothing! So you've no tools, no money for the fine, and you've got to get back to Santa Maria?

PRIEST. Yes, Lieutenant.

LIEUT. And when you are there, have you planted your crops yet?

PRIEST. It's bad soil between the marshes and the mountains.

LIEUT. Your daughter—I remember your daughter. You should be thinking of her future.

PRIEST. It's hard to make a living out of stones.

LIEUT. Then go across the mountains. In the next State the soil's good. And they suffer idlers more than I do here. (*Goes up Right.*)

PRIEST. Always people tell me to go away.

LIEUT. They know better than you do then. Take their advice.

PRIEST. Yes. Yes. I will.

LIEUT. How will you get food on the way home?

PRIEST. I've begged before now. (*Left Center.*)

LIEUT. (*Taking coins from pocket.*) We won't have

beggars in this State. (*Right of him.*) Take this—and if there's any over, buy a bit of chocolate for your daughter, to show you haven't forgotten her in the city.

PRIEST. (*Looking at the money in his palm.*) You mean—I can go?

LIEUT. That's what I said. Go where the land is good and you can find work. (*He turns away—opens door.*)

PRIEST. Lieutenant. (*Up to door.*)

LIEUT. Well?

PRIEST. You are a good man. (*Goes out of door and round grille to Down Right.*)

LIEUT. You don't need to thank me. Just go away and don't come back. Promise me that. (*Following him. The* PRIEST *nods humbly. He can't trust his voice. He crosses to Center of forestage.*) What's the matter with you, man? You are free to go. (*He goes to him, turns the* PRIEST'S *face. He looks closer and wipes away tear.*) Are you still drunk?

PRIEST. The soil is bad.

LIEUT. I know.

PRIEST. I'm going away, I'll never come back, but this soil, this bad soil, I loved it. (*He turns and leaves, going Left Downstage. The* LIEUTENANT *looks after him.*)

CURTAIN

ACT III

SCENE NINE

A village over the frontier. Noon.

The back room of a general store which also serves as a cafe. Through doors at the back we see the shop with its display of goods. Advertisements for aperitifs and liqueurs, an old-fashioned WIRELESS set on a shelf playing music, three or four tables. A large mirror engraved with an advertisement for cognac. Door at Left. SCHOOLMASTER *Right by table.* OBREGON *by counter Left Center. Outside in the street we can hear CHILDREN'S VOICES chanting and the chatter of many VOICES. It sounds like a procession. The CHANTING comes nearer and stops. More CHATTER. The procession enters Up Left. A saint is carried by bearers. The procession crosses slowly across the back of the Stage and exits Down Right followed by the PRIEST in vestments. As the procession disappears Down Right followed by some of the VILLAGERS, OBREGON speaks.)*

OBREGON. It's a fine procession—considering we're out of practice. (*The* SCHOOLMASTER *doesn't answer.*) A cognac?

S'MASTER. No.

OBREGON. Coffee? (*Down Left to packing case.*)

S'MASTER. No.

OBREGON. (*Opening packing case.*) You should enjoy yourself. You've a holiday you weren't expecting.

S'MASTER. My school's been closed so the village may celebrate the feast of St. Agnes. (*Rises violently.*) D'you think it's a holiday for me to see the children go back a thousand years? (*Goes down to Right end of table.*) Now we've a priest there won't be a week when the school

61

isn't closed for some ascension, assumption, circum-
cision- —

(*The* VILLAGERS *return and come into the store.* OBRE-
GON'S WIFE *goes to behind counter.* OTHERS *sit at
the table, lean on the rails, the* INDIAN *squats on the
floor Down Left. They are served with drinks, lemonade, coffee, etc.*)

OBREGON. He's had a hard time. No feast days where
he comes from. And the people like it.

S'MASTER. You too, Obregon. It's good for trade. (OB-
REGON *switches on the wireless.*) Communion wine at ten
pesos the bottle, and half the village drunk by the evening. And that means a bit of extra fornication to tickle
his ears at confession. (*The* CHILDREN *cross and go out
of door Left.*) The church has a bell, and the children
judge the time by the height of the sun.

(OBREGON *rises and takes bottle from packing case to behind the counter.*)

FARMER'S WIFE. They say when they rang the bell this
morning, the rope broke twice.

ALVAREZ. They had to get a new one. Ten metres of
rope at a peso the metre. Who's going to pay for it?

(ALVAREZ *and a* VILLAGER *go to the bench Down Left
Center and start to play crap.*)

S'MASTER. (*Sits Left of table.*) Who do you think will
pay for it? We will, of course. Now it'll start all over
again—Guild of the Blessed Sacrament, Children of
Mary—collecting boxes, subscriptions, bazaars, all the
rest of it.

FAR. WIFE. The Father's not staying. He leaves after
the baptisms.

S'MASTER. I thought as much. No priest ever stays long
up here. No fat pickings.

OBREGON'S WIFE. He has to go to see the Bishop at Las Casas.

S'MASTER. Yes! Las Casas. That's a paradise for priests. There are more priests in Las Casas than in Rome.

OBREGON'S WIFE. He has to see the Bishop, hasn't he? He can't take an empty church without permission.

S'MASTER. Anyone like to take a bet? I'll lay ten pesos to one he never comes back. Not after he's tasted the cooking in Las Casas. (*The* CHILDREN *enter Up Left with skeleton puppets which they dance across the stage.* RAMON *is stopped by the* SCHOOLMASTER.) Ramon. Have you done the task I set you? Don't pretend you've forgotten. To write out the theorem of Pythagoras two hundred times.

RAMON. No. I haven't—yet.

S'MASTER. It's to be done by tomorrow. Don't forget.

(CHILDREN *go out Up Left.*)

FARMER'S WIFE. You're too hard on them—

S'MASTER. (*Rises to Center.*) Perhaps you'd rather have a priest to teach them. Let them learn about Peter and Paul instead of Pythagoras. And then they can recite the Credo, and can't measure their fields. Do you know why this State is so backward? Because the priests are still here and we haven't a Governor with the courage to exterminate them as they do over the frontier.

(*The* PRIEST *appears Up Right. He carries the vestments he has had on for the procession. He is transformed. Already he seems fatter, calmer, and the vestments give him a new dignity.* OBREGON *switches off the* WIRELESS. *The* SCHOOLMASTER *stops, conscious that he has lost his audience. Everyone is looking at the* PRIEST. ALL *rise. The* PRIEST *comes in. The* FARMER'S WIFE *and* OBREGON'S WIFE *kiss his hand,* ALVAREZ *takes off his hat.*)

PRIEST. Well, my children—you were glad to come to your church again? (*He motions them to sit.*)

ALL. Yes, Father. Yes!

PRIEST. (*Center.*) And the procession went well, didn't it? I'm glad your children can still sing Ora pro nobis. It was nice that my first day here should be a feast day, and we could make a show. You must put these away. (*Hands vestments to* OBREGON'S WIFE.)

OBREGON'S WIFE. (*Right of him.*) I've kept them in the chest for three years, just for the day when a priest could come to us. We couldn't leave them in the church, they'd have rotted away.

PRIEST. You keep them in camphor?

OBREGON'S WIFE. (*Folding them.*) Yes, Father, and the chest's sandalwood, so there's no fear of moth. (*She is folding the vestments. The* PRIEST *stops her.*)

PRIEST. No! That way you may break the gold thread. Let me show you. (*He folds them on a bench Left Center, lovingly caressing the silk. He watches her take them away. He is dressed in a plain dark suit. He turns to the* OTHERS.) What time is it?

OBREGON. Just after five, Father.

PRIEST. Ah—no wonder I'm so hungry.

(OBREGON'S WIFE *exits Left with vestments.*)

OBREGON. There's something cooking for you now. Would you like some coffee while you wait?

PRIEST. Yes, please. (*Sits Left of table.* OBREGON *goes to counter. The* VILLAGERS *group round him. The* CHILDREN *in front.*) Well, well—I seem to know you all already—as though I'd been here for years. You're Vittorio.

VITTORIO. (*Right.*) Yes, Father.

PRIEST. Are my mules ready?

VITTORIO. Ready whenever you like, Father.

PRIEST. And you're—Alvarez? Is that right?

ALVAREZ. (*Left.*) Right first time, Father! (*Rises.*)

PRIEST. (*Rises.*) It was you who lent me these clothes. I haven't thanked you. How do you think they suit me?

ALVAREZ. A bit on the large size, Father. But that's my fault, not yours.

(OBREGON *comes Down with the coffee. The* PRIEST *stands stirring the cup. He might be in the parish hall.*)

PRIEST. Thank you, Obregon. Well, well—when I got here the day before yesterday I thought I must have worn my feet to the bone. Plod, plod, plod— I wonder how many miles I covered. (*Sits.*)

FARMER'S WIFE. (*Brings packing case to his Left, sitting.*) Were you alone, Father? All the time?

PRIEST. Yes. Except that just the other side of the pass I met an Indian woman. She had a sugar loaf, and she broke off a piece and gave it to me. That was all I had for two days. She saved my life—and I didn't even know her name. I slept in an Indian hut at the top of the pass, and when I woke up she had gone. But she'd left me the other half of the sugar loaf. That lasted me till I came here. (*He sips the coffee.*) Which shows that the traveller who trusts in God will always arrive at his journey's end.

S'MASTER. Sermon over. In the name of the Father, the Son and the Holy Ghost.

(OBREGON'S WIFE *enters with tray of food which she puts in front of* PRIEST.)

OBREGON. And now you've the journey to Las Casas.

PRIEST. Yes. It's two days, you say?

VITTORIO. Two, perhaps three.

OBREGON. Just wait till you get there. That's a real town—electric light, trams, two hotels. And the cathedral —it's so big you could put this village inside it.

PRIEST. (*A luxurious little chuckle.*) Aha— (*He finishes his coffee.*) Well, for ten years I've had faith. I knew things would turn out right in the end. And here and there I've been able to do a little good—say a Mass, or hear a confession. I expect it's been for the best after all.

ALVAREZ. You don't think—

PRIEST. What, Alvarez?

ALVAREZ. You don't think—we could have another Mass, Father. Tomorrow, perhaps?

PRIEST. But—it's not possible, you see. I have to go.

FARMER'S WIFE. Of course, Father.

VITTORIO. (*After a silence.*) All the same, at Las Casas they don't need you. Not like we need you here.

PRIEST. You mean, there are enough priests in Las Casas already?

VITTORIO. Yes, Father.

PRIEST. (*A touch of sharpness.*) There can never be too many.

VITTORIO. I didn't say that, Father.

(OBREGON *to back of counter.*)

PRIEST. It was what you meant. . . . (*He casts about for a defence.*) Where I have come from, there are no priests. None at all. You know that, but you don't want to believe it. But I've been there, and I know. No priests, no churches, no Masses. Here this morning, I said Mass in a church. You gave me vestments, you rang the bell, you had the proper candles on the altar. You can't know what it meant to me: the first Mass I've said for ten years without being afraid. (*Yet he is conscious that still he has not convinced them. He looks from one face to another, seeking support.*)

INDIAN. You were the only priest in the State? (ALL *look at him.*)

PRIEST. Yes. (*Looks at him.*)

INDIAN. Then why didn't you stay?

(*A pause.* SCHOOLMASTER *laughs. The* PRIEST *looks at him indignantly.*)

PRIEST. It's—it's easy enough to talk. You forget that

—that a priest's first duty may sometimes be to keep himself alive. (*A MURMUR of agreement. Rises to Center.*) When I crossed the frontier, do you think I did so without some—some plan? You know nothing of what goes on over there. Even the Bishop is uninformed—it is my duty to report to him, to enlighten him. And then he and I can sit down and organize . . . organize for the future. The facts must be made known. (*Directly to the* INDIAN, *raising his voice.*) Do you understand what I am saying? (*These fictions have had their effect.*)

OBREGON. You mustn't blame him, Father.

PRIEST. I don't blame him. We can't expect wisdom from the ignorant. (*Sits.*)

OBREGON's WIFE. Of course not, Father. Now finish it up while it's hot.

(OBREGON *pushes* INDIAN *off Left. The* PRIEST *looks round. He has won back his audience. Satisfied, he begins to eat again.*)

PRIEST. When do the rains begin up here?

OBREGON. (*Center.*) Any day now. You can feel it in the air.

PRIEST. Not before I get to Las Casas?

OBREGON. You've no time to lose, Father. If you don't want to be stuck on the way. It floods quickly in the mountains.

PRIEST. (*Concerned.*) Perhaps I'd better leave earlier.

VITTORIO. Not till after the Baptisms?

PRIEST. We could start them earlier—begin at once—

VITTORIO. I've a child to be baptized, Father—

PRIEST. I'll do yours first, then you can bring round the mules while I do the others. (*He is hurrying his meal.*) And the rest of you—there's no time to waste—have all the children ready for me. If anyone's late I shall be gone. (EVERYONE *hurries out, except the* SCHOOLMASTER *and* OBREGON. *To* ALVAREZ.) I must give you back your clothes.

ALVAREZ. It doesn't matter, Father.

PRIEST. (*Rises.*) No, no, no—I couldn't hear of it.

ALVAREZ. I haven't worn them for years—not since I was married. Father, you haven't anything. I'd like to give them to the Church.

PRIEST. (*Very moved.*) Alvarez . . . That's good of you. . . . If—when I come back, I'll repay you.

ALVAREZ. Yes, Father.

(ALVAREZ *goes.* OBREGON *switches on WIRELESS.*)

S'MASTER. Obregon, can I have another lemonade—on credit too?

(OBREGON *brings some cigars from the counter. The* PRIEST *hesitates, then takes one.* SCHOOLMASTER *sits Down Left of counter.*)

PRIEST. (*Right Center.*) Thank you. (OBREGON *takes one too, and lights them both.*) Thank you. (*They puff in silence.*)

OBREGON. (*Left Center, gives the* PRIEST *a newspaper.*) You'll be glad to get away, Father?

PRIEST. Oh, I've been very happy here. And you've looked after me so well. But . . . once one's started a journey one's glad to get to the end.

OBREGON. If you see a Father Quintana in Las Casas, you'll give him my regards?

PRIEST. Quintana. Of course.

OBREGON. And if there's anything you need, there's another friend of mine—dos Santos. He runs a store in the square by the cathedral. Just mention my name.

PRIEST. Thank you.

OBREGON. Obregon.

PRIEST. (*Crosses Down Left Center.*) I hadn't forgotten it. (*Sits bench Down Left Center.*)

OBREGON. No. Your job's like mine. Got to remember people's names—they like it. You're good at that, I noticed. (*The* PRIEST *finds him a little too familiar. A* PEASANT WOMAN *appears in the doorway. She is very poor, very tired, very timid. Brusquely.*) What do you want?

PEASANT WOMAN. Is it true the priest is here?

OBREGON. Well— (*Goes to counter.*)

PRIEST. Yes, I'm here. (*The* PEASANT WOMAN *runs to him, kisses his hand. To his Right.*) What can I do for you?

(OBREGON *switches off the WIRELESS.*)

PEASANT WOMAN. I live a long way off, Father. I heard about the baptisms, and I've brought my two children—

PRIEST. Take them down to the church and I'll do them in their turn.

PEASANT WOMAN. Are you starting soon, Father?

PRIEST. At once.

PEASANT WOMAN. But there are other people coming. From all the villages they're bringing their children— some of them won't be here before night—

PRIEST. I can't wait for everyone. Go and bring your children to the church.

PEASANT WOMAN. (*Crosses to him.*) Father—

PRIEST. Well, what is it?

PEASANT WOMAN. How much must we give you, Father?

PRIEST. (*A puff of the cigar.*) The same as usual. Two pesos.

PEASANT WOMAN. Two— We're very poor, Father.

PRIEST. The Church is poor too, my child. Two pesos is the usual fee.

PEASANT WOMAN. But that's four pesos for the two! We can't afford it, Father.

S'MASTER. (*Comes between them.*) We charge them nothing at the school. (*Crosses Down Right.*)

PRIEST. (*Sharply to* SCHOOLMASTER.) I have to travel to Las Casas. I have to pay the hire of two mules and a guide. I have to pay for my board and lodging here. (*The* SCHOOLMASTER *walks away Down Right. The* PRIEST

looks at the PEASANT WOMAN. *A silence. He hesitates.*)
How many baptisms do you suppose there will be?

PEASANT WOMAN. In the village they say there are
nearly a hundred, Father.

PRIEST. A hundred? M'm . . .

PEASANT WOMAN. And then there are those from outside—

PRIEST. (*To himself.*) One hundred—that's two hundred pesos. Guide and the mules, fifty . . . Mass yesterday . . . Set myself up at Las Casas. Yes. All right—
one peso fifty each.

PEASANT WOMAN. One peso, Father. Please—one peso.

PRIEST. No. One peso fifty.

PEASANT WOMAN. (*Giving in.*) One peso fifty, Father—

PRIEST. Good. Fetch the children—and the money.
Quickly! (*The* PEASANT WOMAN *goes Up Center to
Right.*) I'm sorry.

OBREGON. (*Coming Down with brandy bottle and two
glasses.*) It's the only way, Father. I know them. It's just
the same in my business—they'll never understand that
we have our expenses too.

PRIEST. Are they very poor up here?

OBREGON. (*Right of him.*) So they like to make out.
But whenever they die there's always something tucked
away. (*He rises, fetches a bottle of cognac and two
glasses.*) After all, you're no richer than they are. And
they never value what they don't have to pay for. A drop
of brandy? (*He fills two glasses. The* PRIEST *feigns not
to notice.*) I know them only too well. When we had a
priest here, I was treasurer of the Guild. The trouble I
had to collect their subscriptions! Your good health, Father. (*They drink, the* PRIEST *absently.* MESTIZO *enters
Up Left, crosses back and sits Right of table.*) It's good
stuff. You like it? (*The* PRIEST *doesn't answer.*) You said
yesterday you liked it.

PRIEST. (*Coming out of a dream.*) It's very good.

OBREGON. (*Sitting Right of him.*) I thought perhaps
you'd like a few bottles for your journey. With the mules

to carry it, you could take a dozen if you wanted to. How about—sixty pesos the dozen, say?

(*The* MESTIZO *has entered and sat himself at table Right.* NEITHER *notices him.*)

PRIEST. (*A smile.*) You forget how poor I am.

OBREGON. But a hundred baptisms—at two pesos—

PRIEST. At one fifty. (*Puts newspaper on bench.*)

OBREGON. One hundred at one fifty, that's a hundred and fifty pesos. Guide and mules fifty, that leaves a hundred. Twelve bottles at sixty the dozen—that leaves you forty pesos when you get to Las Casas.

PRIEST. (*Tempted.*) But—I shall have to buy shoes.

OBREGON. Ask, and they shall be given you. They're nice people in Las Casas.

PRIEST. (*After a pause.*) After all, I don't need a dozen bottles.

OBREGON. Ah! Say six then, at five pesos. That's forty pesos.

PRIEST. Thirty pesos.

OBREGON. I tell you what I'll do—I'll make it twenty-five pesos for the six. Twenty-five! Oh, it's a sacrifice! I'll be losing on the deal!

PRIEST. Then why do you sell?

OBREGON. Because, between you and me, that isn't strictly true. (BOTH *laugh.* OBREGON *rises to Up Left, sees* MESTIZO.) What do you want?

MESTIZO. I want to speak to the Father alone.

OBREGON. (*To the* PRIEST.) Do you know the fellow?

PRIEST. Yes, I know him. Let him speak to me.

(*A pause. The* PRIEST *and the* MESTIZO *look at one another in silence.* OBREGON *senses that he is not wanted.*)

OBREGON. I'll see you at the church then, Father. You won't forget that they're waiting for you? (OBREGON *goes out, with an interested backward glance, Up Center to Right.*)

PRIEST. (*Calm, resigned, yet he speaks with a shade of irony.*) I thought—somehow—I should see you again.

MESTIZO. Yes, Father.

PRIEST. Have you brought the Police with you?

MESTIZO. (*Rises.*) What sort of man do you think I am, Father?

PRIEST. One who loves money.

MESTIZO. I'm here—on an errand of mercy. You're the only priest this side of Las Casas. A man is dying. Lopez. (*Crosses to him and sits Right of him.*)

PRIEST. Lopez?

MESTIZO. You met him in prison. He was there for murder.

PRIEST. Someone said his mother was a whore. Yes, I remember.

MESTIZO. He escaped. They shot at him and he was wounded. Now he's dying.

PRIEST. He's not a man who would ask for me.

MESTIZO. Oh, yes. He's a good Catholic, Father.

PRIEST. How do you know he wants me?

MESTIZO. (*Takes a scrap of paper from inside his shirt. The* PRIEST *reads it.*) You can see the blood on it, Father. I'm only an ignorant man, Father. I can't read or write. So I don't know what it says. But he put it in my hand and said, "If you can find the priest, give him this, and tell him where I am."

PRIEST. (*Reading.*) "Father, for Christ's sake come."

MESTIZO. You see?

PRIEST. (*Rises, crosses Right Center.*) How did you meet him?

MESTIZO. I left the prison just after he escaped. (*Rises.*) He was hiding in the town. (*Crosses to Left Center.*) He asked me to help him. And even though he's a murderer, I couldn't refuse to help him, could I? You see, I'm a Catholic, too. You believe me, don't you, Father?

PRIEST. No. (*Throws paper away and sits Left of table Right Center.*)

MESTIZO. No. Any excuse is better than none. And you want to get to Las Casas and sit in the cafes and ride on the trams and have people touch their hats to you in the street. And so you don't want to believe me. (*Steps Upstage.*)

PRIEST. Where is he dying?

MESTIZO. (*To him.*) At the dentist's. The English dentist.

PRIEST. What's he doing there?

MESTIZO. He was trying to leave the country. But he'd lost too much blood.

PRIEST. (*Suddenly angry.*) What sort of a fool do you take me for? The Police can't cross the frontier, they send you over with this as a bait to bring me back.

MESTIZO. (*Going round Upstage table to Right of it.*) That's what you'll say to yourself when you get to Las Casas. But will you tell it to the other priests, Father? That you wouldn't go to a dying man because you thought there might be danger? And so you left Lopez to die in mortal sin? Of course there's danger, but no more than before. I wouldn't lie to you, Father. . . . (*Right of table. His whine trails into silence. The CHURCHBELL begins to ring for the baptisms.*)

OBREGON. (*Enters Up Right. Crosses to Center.*) We're waiting for you, Father. You should see the children! A hundred and twelve! A good thing the rains are coming—we'd be short of water after so many baptisms.

PRIEST. (*To the MESTIZO.*) You see? I have my problems of conscience. Over there, a dying man. Here, a hundred and twelve waiting to be baptized. What would you do if you were me?

MESTIZO. (*After a pause.*) The children have more time, Father.

PRIEST. A good answer. (*Pause. He looks at MESTIZO, then at OBREGON—another pause—he turns to OBRE-*

GON.) I'll take two bottles for ten pesos. (*He is taking the coins from his pocket as:*)

BLACKOUT

SCENE TEN

Outside the Dentist's Surgery

There are the PASSERS-BY *going about their business. The pavement is fairly full. Presently two* POLICEMEN *enter from Left carrying a body wrapped completely in a red blanket; it is* LOPEZ. *They move to Center. Most of the* MEN *raise their hats thinking the man is dead. One or two of the* GIRLS *furtively cross themselves. A third* POLICEMAN *follows the others, he is rough with the crowd, as they* ALL *get to Left Center the* "BODY" *struggles to free himself. The third* POLICEMAN *quickly moves forward and strikes a heavy blow through the blanket at* LOPEZ' *head.* LOPEZ *ceases to struggle. There is consternation in the crowd and the* POLICEMEN *hurry the body off Right. The third* POLICEMAN *starts dispersing the* CROWD *and they begin to move away off Left. A fourth* POLICEMAN *comes in from Right moving the* CROWD *on and handling them roughly. The* CROWD *disperses and the stage is clear except for one* MAN *that lingers in the entrance Left. The fourth* POLICE-MAN *crosses the stage from Right, approaches the* MAN *and hits him very hard in the stomach. The* MAN *reels and moves off Left followed by the* PO-LICEMAN.

BLACKOUT

(*MUSIC is played throughout.*)

SCENE ELEVEN

The dentist's surgery is in darkness. Two Figures *pass the window. The* Priest *gets to the doors, pauses, and enters; he stumbles as he does so.*

Mestizo. You're drunk, Father. (*The* Mestizo *follows him in. He carries a sack containing one empty brandy bottle and one one-third full.*)

Priest. (*Goes to cabinet, he looks round.*) Where is he?

Mestizo. (*Putting sack down Up Left of dental chair.*) I swear I left him here, Father.

(*Suddenly there is a metallic sound from the direction of the dental chair. Both men stiffen.* Lopez, *still covered by the red blanket, painfully crawls from behind the chair to Left Center.*)

Mestizo. Look, Father.

Priest. (*Comes forward, kneels by him and holds him in his arms. Wearily businesslike.*) Your name is Lopez?

Lopez. (*Weakly.*) Who are you?

Priest. A priest.

Lopez. Priest? What priest?

Priest. You sent for me. (*To* Mestizo *who is Up Right.*) Get out and stay out. (Mestizo *goes and stands outside window gazing in.*) I've come to hear your confession, Lopez.

Lopez. All I want is to be left alone.

Priest. When did you last go to confession?

Lopez. I can't remember. Years— I've forgotten what to do.

Priest. You only have to tell—everything you can remember. You're lucky you have a Priest, Lopez. Not many have that now. Do you understand what I'm saying? Just move your head if you do.

LOPEZ. (*With an effort.*) Take my gun, Father. Under my arm.

PRIEST. I've no use for a gun.

LOPEZ. Yes, you have—here, take it— (*He tries to struggle upright.*)

PRIEST. (*Sharply.*) Lie still! Your gun's not there.

LOPEZ. They don't care about me—clear out, it's you they're after. (*Starts to fall.*)

PRIEST. (*Holds him.*) Listen, Lopez. I've come a long way for your sake. I've left a lot of people who needed me. Just think of one thing with sorrow. That's enough. One thing.

LOPEZ. One— (*He is very weak.*)

PRIEST. One, Lopez, one.

LOPEZ. My gun. (*He heaves himself up, struggling with the* PRIEST.)

PRIEST. Lopez, I'm going to have your confession.

LOPEZ. The bastards— (*Struggling forward.*) God damn— (*He collapses into the* PRIEST'S *arms.*)

MESTIZO. (*Hurries into the room and comes Down Left of them. Bending over him.*) He's dead, Father. Dead in his sins. Dead with a curse on his lips.

PRIEST. (*Turning on him in sudden fury.*) He was trying to save me, wasn't he? That's charity. And you?

(*A pause. The* PRIEST *folds* LOPEZ' *arms and says the words of the Conditional Absolution. Suddenly the LIGHTS in the room come on. The* LIEUTENANT *is standing in the doorway, Right, his hand on the switch.*)

LIEUT. Have you finished?

PRIEST. He's dead.

LIEUT. Surprised to see me?

PRIEST. No—I'd like to thank you. (*Rises.*)

LIEUT. What for?

PRIEST. For leaving me alone with him. Long enough. (*To Left of chair.*)

LIEUT. I'm not a barbarian. (*Goes to doors Up Left*

Center. Calling through the door.) Corporal! (*The* COR-
PORAL *enters with* TWO MEN *and* LOPEZ *is carried out. To
the* CORPORAL.) Get rid of the body. (*The* CORPORAL *goes
out.*) You can sit if you want to. I've sent for the truck.
They won't be long. (*To Up Right Center.*)

(*The* PRIEST *sits in the dentist's chair. The* MESTIZO
lingers. He hesitates by the dentist's chair.)

MESTIZO. Father. (*To Left of him.*)
PRIEST. What is it? Haven't you done enough?
MESTIZO. You always think the worst of people, Fa-
ther. There's not much charity in you, is there? I just
want your blessing, that's all.
PRIEST. What good would it be to you? You can't sell
blessing.
MESTIZO. We won't see each other again. I don't want
you to go off thinking ill things.
PRIEST. You are so superstitious. You think my bless-
ing will be a blinker over God's eyes. If you feel sorry,
give away the money—
MESTIZO. What money? There you go again, Father.
PRIEST. (*Wearily.*) All right. I'll pray for you.

(*The* MESTIZO *goes. The* LIEUTENANT *closes and lowers
the blinds. The* LIEUTENANT *goes over to the sack
and opens it.*)

LIEUT. Brandy. Do you need some?
PRIEST. Isn't it against your law?
LIEUT. You're afraid, aren't you?
PRIEST. Of course.
LIEUT. We allow it to the dying. (*He fills a beaker from
the cabinet. They look at one another in silence. Then
the* PRIEST *drinks. The* LIEUTENANT *goes round to Right
of chair—he places bottle on floor.*) Better? (*The* PRIEST
holds out the beaker again. It is filled and he drinks. The
PRIEST *looks at his hand. It is shaking. He fastens it be-*

tween his knees.) You all the time. In the village, in the prison. (*Behind to Center.*)

PRIEST. Yes.

LIEUT. And you've got a child?

. PRIEST. You mustn't think they're all like me. There are good priests and bad priests. It's just that I'm a bad one. (*He puts a hand to his pocket.*)

LIEUT. Humility.

PRIEST. Oh, no. To be humble you have to have virtue and feel no pride in it. I have no virtue. I am not an interesting man, Lieutenant.

LIEUT. (*Sharply.*) Keep your hand away from your pocket!

PRIEST. It's only a pack of cards. I thought it would help to pass the time.

LIEUT. (*Impatiently.*) I don't play cards.

PRIEST. I'll show you a trick. It's called Fly Away Jack. I cut the pack in three, so. . . . And I take the Jack of Hearts and I put it in the center, so. . . . Now I tap the three: I say "Fly Away Jack . . ." (*He cuts the left-hand pack and produces the Jack.*) And here he is!

LIEUT. There are two Jacks.

PRIEST. See for yourself. (*He reaches out for the brandy and pours himself a third beaker.*)

LIEUT: (*Unable to resist looking.*) I suppose you tell the Indians that that's a miracle of God. (*He gets stool from Up Right and places it Center facing* PRIEST.)

PRIEST. Oh, no. I learnt it from an Indian. I used to do tricks at entertainments in the Parish—for the Guilds, you know, in the old days.

LIEUT. (*Sitting with disgust.*) I remember those Guilds. Children of Mary. St. Agnes. Guild of the Blessed Sacrament.

PRIEST. When you were a boy?

LIEUT. I was old enough to see—

PRIEST. What?

LIEUT. The fake and trickery. Sell all and give to the poor—that was the lesson, wasn't it? And then your committees would get together and the chemist's wife would say: "Oh, such and such a family isn't a deserving case; if they starve it's what they deserve—they're all socialists anyway." And the priest—you—would keep note of who had done his Easter duty and paid his Easter offering. The priest was poor, the church was poor, therefore everyone should sell all and give to the church.

PRIEST. You're right— (*Quickly.*) Wrong too, of course.

LIEUT. What do you mean?

PRIEST. You simplify. Like the saints. When you gave me money at the prison, I knew then you were a good man.

LIEUT. Don't try to flatter me. It's useless. I hear it all day long in the camps and prisons. A man who works in a chocolate factory doesn't eat chocolates.

PRIEST. No.

LIEUT. Why did you come back here? Wasn't the trap obvious? And yet you fell right into it.

PRIEST. I didn't fall. I came into it. It was not you who set it.

LIEUT. Who?

PRIEST. I've dreamt a long time of being at peace with God and myself. Now I am—except for this fear. (*He drinks.*)

LIEUT. (*Angry because he can't help liking the man.*) You are going to be a martyr—you've got that satisfaction. (*Rises to Left Center.*)

PRIEST. Oh, no, martyrs are not like me. They don't think all the time—if I hadn't drunk so much brandy I would be on my knees begging you for life.

LIEUT. I had twelve hostages shot because of you. They were my own people. I wanted to give them—the whole world.

PRIEST. Perhaps that's what you did. Tell me! You hate the rich and love the poor. Is that right?

LIEUT. Yes.

PRIEST. And you wanted to give them the world. Well,

if I hated a man I wouldn't want to bring up my children to be like him. It isn't sense.

LIEUT. (*Above chair to Right.*) You're twisting my meaning. If people like you see someone in pain all you can do is reason, "Perhaps pain is a good thing, perhaps it will do you good." I don't want to reason—I want to let my heart speak.

PRIEST. At the end of a gun.

LIEUT. Yes. At the end of a gun.

PRIEST. (*Tilting the bottle to make sure it is empty.*) Perhaps when you are my age you will know the heart's untrustworthy—love—a girl puts her head under water, or a baby is strangled, and the heart all the time says love.

LIEUT. You say all that to *me* but to someone else you say God is love.

PRIEST. Oh, that's another matter. God *is* love but you and I wouldn't recognize that love. It might even look like hate. It set fire to a bush in the desert and set the dead walking. A man like you would run a mile sooner than face that kind of love.

LIEUT. (*Slowly crosses below to stool, almost as though he wanted to comfort.*) I have nothing against you as a man. (*Turns to him.*)

PRIEST. (*Fiercely recovering.*) Oh, yes, you have. I'm made in God's image, aren't I? You've destroyed all the crucifixes and the holy statues but then you look in your mirror when you're shaving and there's the image of God. (*He begins to stretch his arms.*)

LIEUT. (*Sharply.*) What are you doing?

PRIEST. The brandy makes me sleepy, that's all. When you're tired you make a crucifix too.

LIEUT. You're playing with words, aren't you? But what has your church ever done for the people of this country? Did your bishops ever excommunicate a landlord for beating his peasant? When he goes to confession what do you say to him? "You must repent, my son. You must try to amend." And the same evening you're dining at his table and it's your duty to forget he has beaten a peasant to death. You talk about your Gospel—that means good news. Well, we have our good news, too. We'll teach people to read and write and use their minds and hands. And the time will come when poverty will be gone, when they won't need to suffer any more. Then they will be able to forget your Kingdom of Heaven. Because their heaven will be here on earth.

PRIEST. But suppose, just suppose the people want to suffer?

LIEUT. A man may want to rape a child. Are we to allow it, because he wants to? Suffering is wrong.

PRIEST. And you, yourself, are suffering all the time. Don't deny it. It's my vocation to read faces.

LIEUT. And it's mine to read hands. Look how yours shake with the fear of going to your loving God. (*Crosses Left Center.*)

PRIEST. (*Pushing table away—suddenly facing him with great earnestness.*) Listen to me! I'm not as dishonest as you think. When I tell people they are in danger of damnation, I'm not telling them fairy stories I don't believe myself. I've failed God worse than any man in this State, so if there's one man here up for condemnation I'll be in the dock beside him at the last day. God will have to damn me too if he damns anyone. I wouldn't want to be different. I just want justice, that's all.

LIEUT. I want justice, too. Justice here and now. (*Sits stool.*)

PRIEST. Does your Chief of Police feel the same way?

LIEUT. We have our weak men just as you have.

PRIEST. There's the difference. You've *got* to have good men—you can't do without them. But there won't always be good men in your party. What happens then? All the old get-rich-quick-anyhow, starving and beating, just the same as before. But it doesn't matter my being a coward and a drunkard and all the rest. I can put God into a man's mouth just the same—and I can give him God's pardon. It wouldn't make any difference to that man if every priest in the Church was as bad as me.

(There is a pause. A TRUCK is heard approaching. The
Lieutenant goes to door and pulls up the blind.
The Corporal enters.)

Corporal. We're ready, Lieutenant.

(The Lieutenant motions the Priest to the door. The
Chief enters and goes Up Right.)

Priest. I'm going to be tried?

Lieut. You have been tried.

Priest. You mean— I thought I had a day or two left.
Time to—

Lieut. You have an hour.

Priest. Please. Just one more drink.

Lieut. *(Picking up the bottle.)* Empty.

Priest. *(Reaches over chair unsteadily for the sack.)*
There must be some more. *(He rummages among the*
provisions. He pulls out a second bottle which is empty.
The door opens and Tench enters slowly. He goes up
Center. The Priest rises, goes up Left Center—somehow
finding his courage and his dignity.) Forgive me, I have
been a danger to you. Please pray for me.

Tench. Pray? Me? *(The Priest turns and goes out*
of the door, preceded by the Corporal, followed by the
Lieutenant. Tench is alone with the Chief. He looks
out of the window. We hear a TRUCK drive away. Tench
goes to cabinet.) What did you want to bring him back
for? You'd driven him over the frontier. You could have
let him live. *(Goes to back of chair.)*

Chief. *(Cross front to Left Center.)* Do you still keep
oil of cloves?

Tench. No. *(Behind chair.)*

Chief. Shall I see you at the cantina?

Tench. No. *(The Chief goes to doors.)* Have you
heard the joke they are telling about the bodies?

Chief. Bodies?

Tench. Somebody found three bodies lying in the
street. People who had been executed. There was a label

on each one. "Shot for capitalist activities." "Shot for befriending priests." "Shot by mistake."

CHIEF. We don't make mistakes here. I come next week for scaling?

TENCH. Of course.

CHIEF. (*Moves to the door.*) Good night. (TENCH *doesn't reply. The* CHIEF *lingers at the door.*) Do you know what I dream sometimes at night? I dream I'm in a country where people take bribes, get drunk after work and have a girl in the corner of a field.

TENCH. It's a sign of age, living in the past. (*The* CHIEF *goes out.* TENCH *switches out the* LIGHTS. *He goes to window and opens the Venetian blind slats. A* FIGURE *is discovered behind it looking in. There is a pause and the* FIGURE *comes in Left Center.*) Who is it?

MAN. (*Hesitatingly.*) Are you the dentist?

TENCH. (*Right Center.*) Yes.

MAN. (*Left Center.*) I've been waiting till they went. I want to see you alone.

TENCH. Oh, I'm alone all right.

MAN. I have an old filling which has worked loose. It needs attention.

TENCH. (*After a pause.*) What have you done? Raped your mother? Broken a bank? Killed a child?

MAN. (*As though giving another password.*) Agnus dei qui tollis peccata mundi.

TENCH. (*After a pause.*) You want to leave the country?

MAN. No—no. I've just come in. A small boat, across the Gulf, I was told you'd help me—to make a start.

TENCH. I— (*He sighs, shrugs, relents.*) Sit down, Father.

MAN. Thank you. (*He sits in the dentist's chair.*)

TENCH. (*Nervously.*) You mustn't come back here. I can't help you. I'm finished. But I can give you an address. . . . (*He goes to cabinet, takes pad and pencil from drawer. He comes back Center and begins to write.*)

SCENE TWELVE

Outside the Dentist's Surgery

The two men have played the previous scene in blue back lighting from the harbor. As TENCH *comes forward with the pad and pencil the Dentista Window flat is lowered, the shutter is up and we see through it the* TWO MEN *in silhouette. They are bending over the swivel table Center as* TENCH *writes and—)*

THE CURTAIN SLOWLY FALLS

(The MUSIC plays until the Curtain is down.)

THE POWER AND THE GLORY

PROPERTY PLOT

SCENE ONE—FRONT STREET

Torches for each of three POLICEMEN
Cigarettes for "TART" and SAILOR

SCENE TWO—DENTAL SURGERY

Down Right: Stove with lid and lifting handle
Above It: Shelf with jar of cotton wool wads, various
  bottles, plaster of paris moulds, towel on nail
Up Stage of Stove: Waste bin
Below Door Right: Light switch
Up Stage of Door: Table with magazines, cap (POLICE
  CHIEF'S)
Up Stage of Table: Fan on stand (not practical)
Across Back Under Window: Bench
Above Window: Practical Venetian blind
Above Door Left Center: Practical Venetian blind
On Wall Up Right: "Southern Railway" poster—"Bog-
  nor"
On Wall Up Left: Coat pegs with revolver in holster on
  belt (POLICE CHIEF'S)
Cabinet Left: Towel, enamel water jug, bottle of "Oil of
  Cloves," 4 tumblers, bottle of "Mouth Wash" tab-
  lets, 4 pieces of dirty cotton wool, bridge samples in
  box lid (top drawer Up Stage), ticket and form (3rd
  drawer down Up Stage), pen, bottle of ink (bottom
  drawer Up Stage), clean neck towel, drills (top
  drawer Down Stage)
Under Cabinet: Vulcanizer, enamel basin, boxes, etc.
  Dressing
Down Stage of Cabinet: Gas equipment—stand, tube,
  bag, cylinder, muzzle piece, etc. Wash basin, soap,
  towel. Enamel bucket under it. Wall mirror above it

Right Center Stage: Dental chair, neck towel on it
Right of Chair: Foot pedal drill, dentist stool
Left of Chair: Swing shelf table with spittoon on bracket
On Table: Tumbler with water containing mouth wash
    jar with mouth mirror, probe, forceps and tooth
Off Up Left: Bottle of ether in straw labelled, cylinder
    of gas—labelled, gold tooth for LIEUTENANT
Off Up Right: Attache case containing: Missal, towel,
    shirt, collar, flat half-size Brandy bottle ⅓ full
Window Blind Down—Slats Open
Door Blind Up—Slats Open

SCENE THREE—FRONT STREET
Chalk for CRIPPLE BOY
Revolver for POLICEMAN

SCENE FOUR—HUT
Curtain to Doorway Right
Wall Down Stage of Door: Loop (to hang shawl through)
Floor Down Stage of Door: Bucket
Up Right: Cupboard with curtain, in it bowl of onions
    and vegetables, knife in bowl. White tablecloth,
    saucer, tin bowl (for collection), 2 candles in tins,
    matches, bread on board, knife on board, 3 cups,
    empty wine bottle
Up Center: Washing in basket: Towel, skirt, sheet, blouse
Up Left: Stove with cooking pot of maize soup, ladle, tin
    plate
Down Stage of Stove: Pitcher of water
Left Center: Table
Right of Table: Stool
Left of Table: Stool
Off Up Left: Attache case (as SCENE TWO) containing
    bottle of wine ⅓ full
Personal: Coin for PRIEST, coins for VILLAGERS, loaded
    revolver in holster for LIEUTENANT

SCENE FIVE—CITY STREET (Illuminated)
Nil

SCENE SIX—HOTEL BEDROOM

Down Right: Column with coat on hook, light switch, light bracket

In Corridor Right: Light bracket

Right Center: Single bed, brass. *On It:* Sheets, pillow, bedspread, 2 magazines, tie, pair trousers

In Box Under Spring Mattress: Two full bottles (square) of Brandy

Over Bed: Mosquito net attached to ceiling

Left of Bed: Table with Gramophone record on it (wound)

Under Table: Pile of records (one to break)

Off Up Center in Bathroom: Chair with towel, light switch, 4 glasses

Window Left Center: Curtain on pole

Under Window: Chair

Up Left: Brass pedestal with Aspidistra

On Wall Above: Shirt on peg

On Wall Left: Mirror, light bracket

Below It: Chair

Down Left Center: Large wicker chair with valance round seat and cushion. In base of chair: Two round bottles of wine

Right of Chair: Table with ledge under it

On Table: Letters, ash tray, pack of cards

Hanging Center of Ceiling: Practical fan

Personal: Coins for PRIEST, cheroot for CHIEF

SCENE SEVEN—CITY STREET (Illuminated)

Bottle of wine for PRIEST (as from previous scene)

SCENE EIGHT—PRISON

In Cell Center: Large bucket Center, bundle Up Left (SPINSTER'S)

Behind Grille Up Center: Table with register, pen, ink

Left of Table: Stool

Off Up Right: Bucket with floor cloth

Personal: For WARDER: Keys, revolver. For LIEUTEN·

ANT: Coin, notebook and pencil. For LOPEZ: Cigarette, matches

SCENE NINE—STORE

Stage Right: Curtained doorway
Down Stage of It: Large pitcher
Up Stage of It: Barrow with vegetable basket, marrow
Right Center on Truck: Form Up and Down Stage
Left of It: Table
Left of Table: Form
Left Center Up Stage: Counter with radio Left End, 4 bottles Coca Cola, 2 bottles lemonade, 2 bottles Brandy, jug of hot coffee, 3 mugs, 6 small glasses, 6 tumblers, newspaper, 2 cigars in box, box of matches, ½ bottle of Brandy, ashtray, vegetable basket
Under Counter: Crate, vegetable basket, jug, small empty crate for sitting on
Down Stage Left Center: Form
Hanging From Ceiling: 4 cauldrons, 2 large jugs
Hanging Back Stage Right Center: Bunches of onions, sign "Cognac," 8 frying pans
Hanging Above Opening Center: Sign cut-out "Obregon" (printed backwards)
Hanging Back Stage Left Center: Sign "Vino Vinto," bunches of onions
Hanging Wall Left: 3 straw hats
Below Door Left: Sign "Cognac" over picture
Under It On Floor: Two barrels
Off Left: Tray with bowl of food, bread on plate, spoon, bottle of lemonade, 2 puppet skeletons for CHILDREN
Personal: Three rattles for CHILDREN, dice and coins for ALVAREZ, bloodstained note for MESTIZO, vestments for PRIEST
Off Up Left: Stretcher bearing Saint Agnes, dressed and jewelled for religious procession

SCENE TEN—FRONT STREET

Red blanket for LOPEZ

SCENE ELEVEN—DENTIST SURGERY

Set As for Scene Two Except: Drill to above door by wall Right. Swing table moved 18 inches to Center. Light switch Up. Waste bin to Up Right of chair

Cabinet Left: 2 tumblers, pad and pencil 3rd drawer down Up Stage

Off Up Right: Sack containing empty Brandy bottle, ⅓ full Brandy bottle, briefcase

Personal: Pack of cards with rubber band for PRIEST

Venetian Blind Over Window: Down with slats open

Venetian Blind Over Door: Up with slats closed

SCENE TWELVE—FRONT STREET

Nil

SCENE WORKING PLOT

SCENE   1. Front cloth French flat. Center window. Window has a shutter which is up. Window is gauzed.

2. The dentist surgery. Boat truck. Ship on harbor backing seen through window and doors.

3. Same as Scene One with shutter down.

4. Half set. Trellised box set. Sky back cloth.

INTERVAL

5. Front cloth. Black velour. Illuminated signs dropped in front of velour.

6. Bedroom on boat truck set towards prompt. Corridor up and down O.P.

7. Same as Scene Five.

8. Prison cell. Grille.

INTERVAL

9. Full set. Cyclorama. Ground row. Store on boat truck.

10. Same as Scene One. Shutter down.

11. Same as Scene Two. Harbor backcloth.

12. Same as Scene One. Shutter UP.

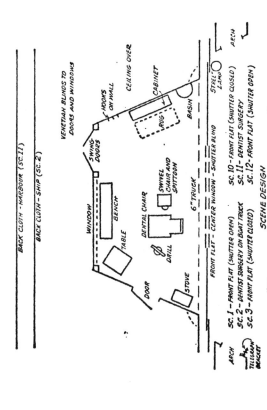

BACK CLOTH - HARBOUR (SC. 11)

BACK CLOTH - SHIP (SC. 2)

VENETIAN BLINDS TO DOORS AND WINDOWS

CEILING OVER

HOOKS ON WALL

CABINET

SWING DOORS

RUG

BASIN

WINDOW

BENCH

TABLE

DENTAL CHAIR

SWIVEL CHAIR AND SPITTOON

DRILL

6" TRUCK

STREET LAMP

ARCH

STOVE

DOOR

FRONT FLAT - CENTER WINDOW - SHUTTER BLIND

SC. 1 — FRONT FLAT (SHUTTER OPEN)
SC. 2 — DENTIST SURGERY ON BOAT TRUCK
SC. 3 — FRONT FLAT (SHUTTER CLOSED)

SC. 10 — FRONT FLAT (SHUTTER CLOSED)
SC. 11 — DENTIST SURGERY
SC. 12 — FRONT FLAT (SHUTTER OPEN)

SCENE DESIGN

"THE POWER AND THE GLORY"

ARCH

TELEGRAM BRACKET

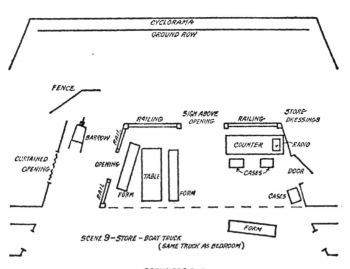

DARK BACKCLOTH WITH ILLUMINATED SIGNS

WINDOW OPENING

CHAIR

BATHROOM

DOOR

OPENING

MOSQUITO NET OVER

WINDOW

SHUTTERS

CURTAIN

PEDESTAL AND PLANT

DOOR

TABLE GRAM.

CHAIR

CHAIR

LIFT DOORS

BRASS BED

LIGHT SWITCH

BLACK VELOUR ILLUMINATIONS

HIGH BACKED CANE CHAIR

TABLE

SCENE 5 - STREET SCENE - ILLUMINATED SIGNS
SCENE 6 - HOTEL BEDROOM - BOAT TRUCK
SCENE 7 - SAME AS SCENE 5

CYCLORAMA

GROUND ROW

FENCE

BARROW

RAILING

SIGN ABOVE OPENING

RAILING

STORE DRESSINGS

RAIL

COUNTER

RADIO

CUSTAINED OPENING

OPENING

TABLE

CASES

DOOR

RAIL

FORM

FORM

CASES

FORM

SCENE 9 - STORE - BOAT TRUCK
(SAME TRUCK AS BEDROOM)

SCENE DESIGNS
"THE POWER AND THE GLORY"

SKY BACKCLOTH — PAINTER GROUNDROW

BACK FLAT & CEILING FLY

CUPBOARD

STOVE

CLOTHES LINE

CURTAINED DOORWAY

CURTAINED DOORWAY

CURTAINED DOORWAY

BUCKET

TABLE

STOOL

STOOL

CEILING

SCENE 4 — HUT-TRELLISED

BLACK VELOUR FLY

OPENING WITH LINEN BACK

ROW TO FLY

ENTIRE UNIT TO FLY

OPEN GRILLE BACK

TABLE

STOOL

FOLDS BACK TO FLY

DOOR

FOLDS BACK TO FLY

FOLDS BACK TO FLY

GRILLE

OPEN GRILLE SIDES

OPEN GRILLE CEILING

BUCKET

OPEN GRILLE SIDES

GRILLE

SCENE 8 — PRISON

SCENE DESIGNS
"THE POWER AND THE GLORY"

THE SCENE
Theresa Rebeck

Little Theatre / Drama / 2m, 2f / Interior Unit Set
A young social climber leads an actor into an extra-marital affair, from which he then creates a full-on downward spiral into alcoholism and bummery. His wife runs off with his best friend, his girlfriend leaves, and he's left with… nothing.

"Ms. Rebeck's dark-hued morality tale contains enough fresh insights into the cultural landscape to freshen what is essentially a classic boy-meets-bad-girl story."
- New York Times

"Rebeck's wickedly scathing observations about the sort of self-obsessed New Yorkers who pursue their own interests at the cost of their morality and loyalty."
- New York Post

"The Scene is utterly delightful in its comedic performances, and its slowly unraveling plot is thought-provoking and gut-wrenching."
- Show Business Weekly

THREE MUSKETEERS
Ken Ludwig

All Groups / Adventure / 8m, 4f (doubling) / Unit sets
This adaptation is based on the timeless swashbuckler by Alexandre Dumas, a tale of heroism, treachery, close escapes and above all, honor. The story, set in 1625, begins with d'Artagnan who sets off for Paris in search of adventure. Along with d'Artagnan goes Sabine, his sister, the quintessential tomboy. Sent with d'Artagnan to attend a convent school in Paris, she poses as a young man – d'Artagnan's servant – and quickly becomes entangled in her brother's adventures. Soon after reaching Paris, d'Artagnan encounters the greatest heroes of the day, Athos, Porthos and Aramis, the famous musketeers; d'Artagnan joins forces with his heroes to defend the honor of the Queen of France. In so doing, he finds himself in opposition to the most dangerous man in Europe, Cardinal Richelieu. Even more deadly is the infamous Countess de Winter, known as Milady, who will stop at nothing to revenge herself on d'Artagnan – and Sabine – for their meddlesome behavior. Little does Milady know that the young girl she scorns, Sabine, will ultimately save the day.

CPSIA information can be obtained
at www.ICGtesting.com
Printed in the USA
BVOW06s1711070817
491176BV00012B/42/P

9 780573 614231